JUN 12 2006

10668189

BE HEARD
THE FIRST TIME

DISCARDED
From Nashville Public Library

Capital Ideas for Business & Personal Development Series

From High Heels to Bunny Slippers: Surviving the Transition from Career to Home by Christine Conners, MA

Million Dollar Networking: The Sure Way to Find, Grow and Keep Your Business by Andrea Nierenberg

More Alive with Color: Personal Colors—Personal Style by Leatrice Eiseman

Nonstop Networking: How to Improve Your life, Luck and Career by Andrea Nierenberg

Now What Do I Do? The Woman's Guide to a New Career by Jan Cannon, Ph.D.

The Power of Handshaking: For Peak Performance Worldwide by Robert E. Brown and Dorothea Johnson

The 10 Lenses: Your Guide to Living & Working in a Multicultural World by Mark A. Williams

Your Identity Zones: Who Am I? Who Are You? How Do We Get Along? By Mark A. Williams

Save 25% when you order any Capital titles from our Web site: www.capital-books.com.

BE HEARD
THE FIRST TIME

The Woman's Guide to Powerful Speaking

Susan D. Miller, PhD, CCC-SLP

CAPITAL IDEAS FOR
BUSINESS AND PERSONAL
DEVELOPMENT

CAPITAL
BOOKS, INC.

Copyright © 2006 by Susan D. Miller

All rights reserved. No part of this book may be reproduced or utilized in any form or by any means, electronic or mechanical, including photocopying, recording, or by any information storage and retrieval system, without permission in writing from the publisher. Inquiries should be addressed to:

Capital Books, Inc.

P.O. Box 605

Herndon, Virginia 20172-0605

ISBN 10: 1-933102-15-2

ISBN 13: 978-1-933102-15-3 (alk.paper)

Library of Congress Cataloging-in-Publication Data

Miller, Susan D.

Be heard the first time : the woman's guide to powerful speaking / Susan D. Miller.-- 1st ed.

     p. cm.

Includes bibliographical references and index.

ISBN 1-933102-15-2 (pbk. : alk. paper)

1.   Public speaking for women. I. Title.

PN4192.W65M56 2006

808.5'1082--dc22

                     2005028633

Printed in the United States of America on acid-free paper that meets the American National Standards Institute Z39-48 Standard.

First Edition

10 9 8 7 6 5 4 3 2 1

Contents

Preface

I grew up in a wonderful, close and supportive, but non-communicative, family with an older and younger brother with whom I constantly competed for attention. Unlike most boys, I "chattered" a bit as a young girl. I don't remember when it was, exactly, but early on it dawned on me that no one was actively listening! As a defense, I began to hold my true thoughts inside. Nevertheless, I grew up to be a normal kid. Active and popular, I was elected vice president of my high school class, which terrified me! I absolutely dreaded public speaking, any sort of debate, and even, at times, simple class participation.

In college, I discovered speech pathology, a profession that taught persons with all degrees of speech and communication handicaps how to express themselves successfully. I learned processes and strategies for helping people comprehend, articulate, and clearly verbalize their central message in any speaking situation. A light bulb within me was illuminated as I learned, first, how to better express myself, and later, how to drastically and permanently transform clients with similar fears. For nearly thirty years now, I have trained clients with many different communication handicaps. I've been trusted to teach my methods and techniques to executives and professional speakers at the highest levels of government, business and the media.

My clients depend on me to help them cope with performance anxiety, and to communicate consciously, clearly and effectively. In response to many of their requests to publish my methods, and with gratitude toward those whose stories I share in this book, I am most privileged to write this book.

This is a practical guide. It presents competencies, strategies and skills employed by the most well-known and very successful speakers of our generation. It teaches seven key skills all competent speakers share. Moreover, the book is intended to be an operator's manual for oral communication.

Introduction

Should you read this book? Before you decide, please review the following remarks and circle "**YES**" if they are, or have ever been, true for you? You may wish to recall your worst communication nightmare. Be as honest as possible. Your future is at stake!

- I know the content of my presentation but lack poise and confidence in my delivery. **Yes**
- I don't know what to do with my hands during a presentation. **Yes**
- I hate the sound of my voice. **Yes**
- I wish that I could stop my voice from shaking and my chest from tightening when I speak before a group. **Yes**
- I can't project my voice in a noisy restaurant. **Yes**
- I dislike impromptu speaking situations. **Yes**
- I say *um* or *like* frequently when I speak. **Yes**
- My voice lacks spontaneity and expression. **Yes**
- I am frequently asked in what part of the country I was born. **Yes**

I don't know what to talk about at a cocktail party.   Yes

I have strong opinions, but rarely express them unless I am called upon to do so.   **Yes**

I find myself nodding my head in agreement when I don't always mean it.   **Yes**

If you answered **YES** to any one of these questions, start reading now! This book is a straightforward operator's guide to learning clear, effective communication. Few of us are born to be excellent communicators. It takes a good coach, practice and a willingness to learn new behaviors.

Just as you struggle learning to hit a golf ball or learning the steps to a dance routine, you must first learn the fundamentals and then rehearse the skills for effective communication in increasingly challenging situations. For a lucky few, presenting speeches and socializing at a cocktail party come naturally, but most of us reach a plateau in our ability or experience stage fright, and never achieve our optimal performance level. Several of you may have suffered a very traumatic speaking incident early in life that paralyzed you and continues to thwart further growth.

Anne, a 31-year-old director of fiscal operations for one of the largest non-profit corporations in Washington, said that she was able to adeptly recite poetry as early as third grade. She remembers loving to speak publicly for large groups of peers and adults until one day, in September of her fifth grade year, when she forgot her lines and her classmates laughed at her. She shut down and refused to present publicly from then on. When she finally decided to seek help following a recent promotion, her speaking rate was extremely rapid with frequently omitted sounds and a monotonous, boring vocal tone. With coaching, she has re-learned how to speak slower with clearer articulation and spontaneous inflection. She has regained her confidence by speaking effectively during several challenging social and work-related interactions.

Anne isn't alone. Many graduates from top universities with high-level corporate or government positions still lack the strategies and competencies needed to communicate successfully at a professional level. A very fundamental problem is, as this book's title states, "being heard." At this most basic level, women and men contact me to teach them to project their voices so that they can be heard in a large conference room. Speaking more loudly is generally not the solution. Training in breath and pitch control, plus attention to posture, presence, comfort level, and the message itself are key ingredients. A company's soft-spoken patent attorney, upon being promoted to president, must quickly learn how to confidently and visibly enter the conference room or reception hall. She must learn to speak quite differently as a corporate executive than she did as a patent attorney. Her first step toward speaking powerfully is to "see" her transformed persona. This is your first step, too. Begin now. "See" the "New You."

I have narrowed mastery of powerful communication into seven key competencies. These are the result of years of work with successful clients. These competencies, illuminated by actual case studies whose names are changed, are presented to you in individual chapters. They include both the nonverbal and verbal aspects of communication and with diligent practice will take you far beyond a public speaking course. We will review the components of physical presence, such as posture and eye communication. We will practice altering breath control, vocal inflection, pausing, and the message itself. You may find that conscious attention to only one or two "keys" may be all that is required to catapult you to the next level!

I hope that you will read this guide with some introspection. Think about how your best, and your worst, communication experiences have gone. Reflect upon the details of why you did well or were disappointed with your performance. You can read this book in one of two ways. You can glance through the chapters and read the italicized pointers to confirm that you have mastered these items and pat yourself on the shoulder. Then, concentrate on the pointers that provide new information. Or, you can delve right into the first chapter and discover what you've been missing.

I promise that if you can employ the pointers displayed in each of the seven chapters on a daily basis for twenty-one days, you will:

- Walk, stand or sit powerfully, even if you feel insecure
- Like the sound of your voice
- Breathe deeply and slowly when you are anxious
- Say the last word of a sentence without trailing off
- Express your opinions, desires, and experiences clearly
- Vary the loudness, pitch, and duration of your voice when speaking
- Entertain others with stories, presentations, and tall tales
- Finish your statement without interruption
- Listen actively without judgment
- Respond assertively to criticism.

SO, LET'S BEGIN!

COMPETENCY 1

ACQUIRING A PROFESSIONAL PRESENCE

"Nervous Nellie/Unkept Ursula"

R alph Waldo Emerson wrote, "What you are speaks so loudly that I cannot hear what you are saying." You may lose credibility within the first few seconds of an interaction if your handshake is weak or if you don't look the person right in the eye during an introduction. We need to be aware of our body language and the nonverbal cues that we may unconsciously send. We can sense displeasure, joy, hurt, and indecision in a friend or colleague simply by her facial expression, posture, body movement, and eye communication. A well-quoted study by Albert Mehrabian, Ph.D. conducted at UCLA in 1981 revealed that over 55 percent of a listener's first impression of a speaker is based solely on body language.

You can likely recall many examples of speakers that you tuned out, or women and men that you didn't approach at a reception, before they ever spoke a word. Unfortunately, these folks unconsciously allowed their bodies to speak for them. I always observe a client before they enter my office. Nervous Nellie sits outside my office with her legs crossed at the knees and again at the ankles. She is dressed professionally with her interview materials in a black leather tote. Her hands are clasped in front of her. Unkept Ursula slumps onto the couch with her interview materials spewing from her small black purse. She never looks at my assistant as she checks in for the appointment. Obviously, Nellie is anxious about the visit; while Ursula lacks self-esteem.

We may not always be correct about our initial impression of a person after our brain receives and understands more information. But that first or "gut" impression is immediate because our primitive brain or limbic system is alerted by early smells, sights, sounds or touches. As our higher brain or cerebral cortex processes additional information, our gut impression may change. If a man dressed in a black shirt and pants walks rapidly towards you, you may be startled until you see his white collar and realize that he is a clergyman. Your gut intuition was fear, and then you understood that he was a priest and calmed down.

Since another's first impression of you is so immediate and significant, you must remain alert. If you wear spicy perfume to a board meeting, others may assume that you view this as a social not a business interaction. If the Chief Information Officer sits with her hands in her lap with her chair slightly back from the boardroom table, she does not appear to be engaged in the discussion at hand and may not be asked for her thoughts about the current budget dilemma.

Discover how easy it is to alter the first message that you deliver to others. Remember, most people are not aware of the signals that they send especially when they are under pressure. Be a detective. Observe yourself for several days during casual, daily situations at home and work, and during intense exchanges in both environments. When you are explicitly aware of your habits, please answer the following questions.

- Do you stand firmly grounded in social situations or do you stand with your hands clasped in front of you, put your hands in your pockets or lean against a nearby wall or table?
- Do your eyes dart to see who has walked by as you speak to your friend or do you maintain eye contact as your colleague expresses her point?

- Do you feel awkward looking directly into a person's eyes during a conversation?
- Do you fiddle with an object when you are uncomfortable?
- Do you find yourself smiling or nodding your head affirmatively when you disagree with the speaker?
- Do you hate dressing professionally on a "casual" Friday?

The good news is that you can't change a behavior until you are aware that it exists! Thankfully, change is quite simple. Study the pointers below and set yourself free! As you "give yourself permission to be more open," you'll walk more freely and easily, swinging your arms as you "glide" along. You will sit leaning forward, with arms on the conference room table or on the arms of your desk chair. You're now "on the playing field; no longer in the stands." AND, listeners will perk up, turn in your direction, and actively hear what you say – the FIRST time!

Assertive Posture

Emerson's words are so true when it comes to our posture. Many women from earlier generations and differing cultures were taught, or unconsciously learned, to occupy minimal space – to remain small. Some women, even today, sit meekly and passively poised, with their arms in their lap, and their feet crossed at their ankles.

This may depend on whether the situation is a personal or business interaction. Years ago, I was one of seven participants in a one-day workshop on public speaking. All of us were medical center faculty members told to make a five-minute presentation which would be videotaped and critiqued by the instructor and course participants.

A meek sitting position implies lack of self-confidence.

I was seated next to a female physician who from the start of the seminar sat twisted like a pretzel. Her long legs were crossed at the knees, ankles, and toes and her fingers continually twirled a pen. I couldn't tell until she introduced herself that she was an accomplished expert in the field of adolescent eating disorders. Her posture during her presentation was confined, with few spontaneous gestures and minimal interaction with the audience. When she was reminded that she was the expert on the topic, and we couldn't tell if she made a mistake, she began to move gracefully and spontaneously. Her confidence soared as the audience became totally immersed in her presentation.

The next time you ride a crowded elevator, observe how many women tend to stand very erect and still. In conferences, receptions and small office meetings, examine whether women sit with their hands folded in their laps or stand with their weight shifted to one side with hands quietly placed together. Do they lean against a wall or table rather than standing firmly planted into the floor? Demure, restricted postures can imply shyness, detachment and lack of self-confidence. I am not asking you to sprawl out as men do in their leather recliner chairs, but be certain to "own your space."

Posture is extremely important for speaking. When standing to speak, be certain that your weight is centered over the balls of your feet and that the weight of your lower body is grounded into the floor, so that someone could not easily push you over. During training sessions, I physically try to push the speaker over as she readies to begin her presentation. In athletic terms, you need to get "ready," just like the stance a basketball player assumes to screen her teammate's shot. Without this grounded stance, your breathing will remain shallow and your voice may quiver as you begin to speak.

Remember, we want to be grounded like a tree with its roots spread and its limbs free to move naturally.

The tree must stand tall. Be certain to stand with your back, neck, and head upright as if a string is attached from the tip of your head through your body down to the balls of your feet. Feel that your head is free and resting comfortably, directly above and between your shoulders, almost suspended like a marionette.

Typically, our shoulders and head roll forward from years of sitting in front of a computer. An excellent exercise to counteract this is to perform a pushup into the inside of an open door jam several times during the day. You also can

A confident, relaxed walking stance.

press your shoulders and head into the headrest of your car during your commute. These simple exercises will stretch out and strengthen your neck muscles.

Rather than thinking of keeping your shoulders erect and back as in a military stance, I find it helpful to ask clients to sit or stand with their necklace or third blouse button or necklace directed upward and forward almost at a thirty degree angle as if this point is the string at the center of a kite. The kite string analogy prevents us from pressing our shoulders backward and up; standing stiff and erect rather than poised and alert.

Walk the same way. Pretend that the kite string is pulling you forward as you glide down the hall. Allow your arms to swing naturally, not confined and held close to your body.

Linda Belans, a presentation trainer, creates the image of a woman with a vase on her head, barefoot, gliding smoothly and powerfully through the sand swinging her arms naturally. Frequently, we find our bodies constricted and tense during the day as we race hurriedly down the hall to a meeting, holding an armful of papers with an overstuffed purse dangling from our elbows. Try to be relaxed as you walk toward the conference room or to your car in the morning. Breathe deeply but naturally through your nose, with smooth, even strides and relaxed forearms, even if you are holding a briefcase, gym bag, or presentation

Smooth, even, confident strides will make you feel positive about yourself.

An upright alert posture implies self-confidence and authority.

handouts. Remember to stride naturally. Your kite string is gently pulling you forward. Especially on a day when you wake up and feel low or rejected, put a bounce in your step and see how positive you feel!

Fortunately, during a confrontation, most women sit in an upright, alert posture rather than reclined in a leather desk chair with our feet on the table or slung over the arm of the chair as men do. However, our upright, constricted posture appears modest and may diminish our influence. Be certain to own your own space. Especially when stressed, sit more forward in your chair with your buttocks firmly planted in the chair and your feet touching the floor. You may want to cross your feet at the ankles. Remember to keep your breastbone in the kite position and your head upright. This posture will assure a deeper, more relaxed breathing pattern that will diminish any vocal quivers and help you to maintain the loudness of your voice. Expand your posture by resting your elbows on the arms of the chair or on the table.

You must remain physically engaged to negotiate your position, rather than retreating physically, before the debate begins.

Assertive Posture Pointers

- *"Own" your space.*
- *Remain fully grounded.*
- *Keep your breastbone forward.*
- *Glide smoothly as you walk.*
- *Allow your arms to swing naturally.*

Unambiguous Eye Communication

If you keep eye contact for a moment until the handshake begins and then quickly look away, what message have you conveyed? If you are conversing with someone at a cocktail party who constantly glances at others as they walk by, how do you feel? Your first real contact in a conversation is eye contact. My first impression of Dr. Peterson, seated demurely beside the conference table, changed immediately when she looked me straight in the eye and clearly defined her objectives. I pay close attention to clients' eye communication with my receptionist when they initially enter the office. Looking away or down may signal shyness, discomfort, guilt, or suspicion while direct eye contact with raised eyebrows suggests friendliness, interest and cooperation. Pay attention to your eye behavior when you first meet a stranger, listen to a colleague, or speak with someone who disagrees with you. Do you maintain eye contact or look away?

Eye Focus

I rarely look someone in the eyes when I speak or listen to them. Instead I focus my eyes on a broader area expanding from the top of their nose to their bottom lip. The speaker or listener has no clue that I am not looking directly into her or his eyes, and it is much more comfortable. Most clients are relieved to hear this and can readily learn this skill. Prolonged, often piercing, eye-to-eye contact frequently occurs during heightened arousal often signaling aggression, hostility or sexual interest. So be certain not to glare at someone when you are listening or speaking to them. This is much less a problem for women who tend to avert their eyes when they feel vulnerable.

If you have difficulty maintaining eye contact during a conversation, first try it when you are listening to a friend with whom you feel comfortable. Since you, the listener, watch more than the speaker does, you will have lots of time to concentrate on looking broadly toward the person's nose and mouth. You may wish to show increased interest by raising your eyebrows or concern by squinting your eyes. When it is your turn to speak, try to maintain eye contact with your friend through a complete thought, which will generally last 3 to 6 seconds. Then feel free to look to one side or down to process your next thought. Don't catch yourself looking upward which signals the need for "divine intervention." When engaged in a group discussion, maintain eye contact through one complete thought with one person and then look toward another listener for the next point.

Your degree of comfort in sustaining eye contact during a verbal introduction and handshake will positively shape your interactions. If you are poised and comfortable during initial introductions, even if you forget the name a second later, you will create an accepting environment for the other person. Frequently during our first meeting, a client will look at me for a split second and then glance away as she says her name. I immediately sense insecurity. It may be the closer proximity of the interaction, or the uncertainty of the scenario, that makes this first handshake and verbal introduction intimidating for some people. Regardless of the reason, practice attaining direct eye communication during introductions until it becomes second nature. Lack of eye communication during a key interview will result in an irreparable first impression even if you are dressed impeccably.

What do you do if a male colleague looks at your body and not at your face during a conversation? Pat Heim in *Hardball for Women*[i] instructed a female vice president of a firm to stop a male colleague from looking at her breasts by pausing mid-sentence as she spoke. As soon as he looked up at her to see why she stopped speaking, she continued speaking. Karen, who is learning to maintain eye contact, learned the hard way by looking too directly at a stranger in the Metro. The stranger yelled, "What are you looking at, lady?" and stomped away. Karen was mortified. She learned quickly that it is best not to maintain eye contact with strangers in public spaces such as stores or on public transportation.

"Eye Dart"

When engaged in a conversation at a cocktail party or crowded reception, be certain to maintain eye contact with your colleague throughout the interaction and don't "eye dart" or glance to see who is passing by. This pattern is rude and disrespectful to your colleague. Mike, a fourth-year medical student, attended the graduation party for the residents. As he engaged in one conversation, his eyes continually wandered to see what was happening around him. Finally, the attractive woman he was speaking to walked away. Mike must learn to focus on the immediate conversation or patients will never feel listened to and heard. Most people who have met former president Bill Clinton mention how intently he listened and spoke to them. When he delivered his second inaugural address, I felt as if he was speaking directly to me. Refined speakers know how to remain totally focused on an interaction and how to verbally make an exit.

It is hard to keep eye contact with the person you are talking to if there is a line of people waiting to speak to you. Learn to focus on one interaction and exit gracefully to the next person. Dr. Kennedy, newly elected president of her professional organization, worked on her address for the annual Internal Medicine Academy meeting. We practiced her presentation but also how to meaningfully, but briefly, interact with each member including what to say to end the conversation and move on to the next well-wisher. This skill takes conscious attention and practice!

Doerthe, a young German woman in Washington, D.C. for a two-year assignment to the German Embassy, came to learn to speak more loudly because her rather aggressive, loud boss could not hear her. Reportedly, when he did hear her ideas, he immediately dismissed them. Doerthe's initial handshake was very weak and she looked downward during our introduction. Although almost six feet tall, she stood with her shoulders rounded and head jutted forward. Our work centered initially on observing the body language of the other women in the embassy. Doerthe saw that the other German women stood tall and looked her boss in the eye when he belted his commands. She realized immediately that her extreme shyness was hindering her success. Doerthe decided to mirror one woman's behavior and soon was able to carry herself more powerfully, look at her boss and be heard – the FIRST time!

Cultural Differences

Patterns of eye communication vary greatly across different cultures. Many Middle Eastern cultures interpret direct eye contact as rude or intrusive. If you typically communicate with a friend or colleague from another country, discuss the accepted norm regarding eye contact. If you will be traveling to another country, be sure to study the internet about the country's nonverbal customs especially regarding handshakes, eye contact, and common gestures that may be interpreted differently. Your preparation will pay off handsomely.

Unambiguous Eye Communication Pointers

- *Focus your eyes on the listener's nose or mouth.*

- *Maintain eye contact through your complete thought.*

- *Avoid "eye dart."*

- *Raise your eyebrows to show interest.*

- *Be cognizant of cultural communication practices.*

Affirming Gestures
and Body Movement

Presentation coaches typically teach lecturers to gesture naturally and spontaneously. A few years ago, I lectured on non-verbal communication for one of the Smithsonian Resident Associate's Programs. Since speakers, when tense, tend to gesture only minimally, I mentioned that gesturing more is better than gesturing less. Ione approached me after the class and told me a personal story. She is a financier from Peru who was asked to speak to a group of American women bankers. Following her lecture, a woman commended her for being fluent in both English and "sign language." Ione was appalled, and learned to reduce hand gestures. Since this conversation, I have modified my comments to clients to: "Be certain that your gestures fit the words and intent of your message."

Phyllis Mindell in *How to Say It for Women* writes that your gestures must match the words, the message, and your character, and they must be natural and not posed. Gestures can be very effective. Kevin Hogan, a corporate public speaking consultant in Minnesota, points out that President George W. Bush frequently uses a "windshield wiper motion," sweeping his right hand from his chest to his side that underscores his heartfelt points. Spencer Kelly, a Colgate graduate who has studied hand gestures, speaks of Clinton's and Kerry's successful use of the "thumb point" with audiences which signals "You are in good hands."

Whether during a presentation or an intimate conversation, gestures should be "kept in front of you; between your shoulders and your waist, within the confines of your body" not "like a whirly bird" outside your body's perimeter. When we are under pressure or feel insecure, interesting body movements and gestures emerge. Many years ago, I held weekly conferences with my department chairman at Georgetown Medical Center. Somehow, in every meeting, I would manage to find a paperclip and twist it incessantly. Only years later did I realize that my discomfort was evident by my fidgeting with the paperclip.

When people are uneasy or stressed, they resort to all kinds of behaviors such as nail biting, face touching, hair twirling, hair smoothing, fiddling with a pen or coin, leg twiddling or foot tapping. Marcia, a non-profit CFO, was horrified when she saw herself on video twirling her hair during a practice session in preparation for an upcoming board meeting. She also tapped her right foot when she was uncertain of an answer. Pat Heim in *Hardball for Women* calls these idiosyncratic behaviors "adaptors," since people utilize them to comfort themselves in tense situations. Once you become conscious of your adaptors, you can begin to gain control of them.

Try to arrange to videotape yourself for several minutes while talking about a familiar subject and then a controversial subject. Be sure to capture your entire body, but zoom in frequently during the review, to record your facial and eye expressions. Review the video first without sound so that you can analyze your body talk. You will become immediately aware of your mannerisms. Review the videotape a second time with the sound and determine which gestures match your message and which are distracting. You may find yourself standing stiffly with your fingers in your pockets or seated rigidly with your hands softly clasped in your lap, or in your pockets if you are standing.

Be certain to allow your hands to fall naturally by your sides or on the arms of the chair. Remember you are expanding into your "own" space, not shrinking into it. If you are very nervous, you can press each thumb into its respective index finger rather than tensing your body. Put your nervous energy into your fingers or into the seat of the chair as you bear down into the chair or into the floor if you are standing. If you like to cross your legs, press the weight of the upper leg into the lower leg. These maneuvers will eliminate your nervous finger rubbing, foot tapping or leg swinging.

If standing and using a lectern during your presentation, place your hands softly on the lectern or by your side so that you are free to gesture. You may wish to use a cordless, multidirectional microphone so that you can move away from the podium to interact with your audience. Be certain not to place a death grip on the sides of the lectern. Dr. Smith, the chairman of orthopedics and the vice president of the Medical Center, lectured to our department one morning. This 6-foot-4-inch man leaned over the podium with his hands outstretched and grasping the front edge of the podium. The faculty seated in the first several rows responded to being "lectured to" by leaning back in their seats.

Affirming Gestures and Body Movement Pointers

- **Gesture naturally.**
- **Match your gestures to your verbal message.**
- **Become conscious of your adaptors.**
- **Videotape yourself and analyze the film without audio.**
- **Transfer your tension to your fingers, buttocks, or legs.**

Engaging Facial Expression

Women will frequently nod their heads up and down or smile to indicate that they are understanding what the person is saying; not nodding to suggest agreement. If this is true of you, be prepared for confrontation if you then vote against the proposal or later object to the advice. Women like to be viewed as team players and want the speaker to know that he or she is being heard, so they frequently acknowledge the speaker with a nod or a verbal *hmmm*.

Carly, the chief information officer for an energy cooperative, attended two briefings prior to her company's accepting a bid for procurement of a badly needed database management system. Management representatives were certain that their system would be chosen because of Carly's big smile and frequently affirming head nod. They were startled and lodged formal protests when Carly accepted the competitor's bid.

Evaluate whether you nod unconsciously or continually smile while listening to someone. If so, become more discriminative and nod or smile only if you definitely agree or do not agree. Raise your eyebrows and lean forward to signify interest or breathe easily as you listen with a more neutral expression on your face. You might tilt your head to one side. Many professionals such as detectives, human resource personnel, attorneys, and counselors are trained to be attentive and interested but minimally expressive in communicating with an individual. Try to analyze the situation beforehand and determine your positions on the issues to be discussed. Then, be conscious of your facial expressions. Are they congruent with your opinions? Does your face reveal a position prematurely when you really want to remain neutral until you make your final decision?

I am not suggesting that you suppress emotion during a communication, but rather that the emotion you express be real. If you are passionate or interested in a subject, show animation while speaking and smile, which will give your voice energy. During the 2004 presidential debates, George W. Bush's initial wide grin diminished as he began to lean forward and narrow his eyes, signifying a sense of compassion when discussing controversial issues such as terrorism and the war in Iraq.

Clients often ask me whether they should change their laugh, especially if it is loud and throaty. Since your laugh is usually spontaneous and generated reflexively from your gut,

Engaging Facial Expression Pointers

- **Match your facial expressions to your intention.**

- **Nod your head or smile discriminately.**

- **Videotape yourself and analyze your facial expression.**

- **Be dynamic and genuine when excited.**

I usually say no, but there are exceptions. Susan was a vice president of finance for a national professional association. She was extremely competent and knowledgeable. In meetings with male superiors, however, she heard herself producing a little nervous laugh. Simultaneously, she would tilt her head to the side and start tapping her foot. Her laugh occurred primarily when she was tense or uncomfortable. This habit was tough to break even though she despised the behavior. Repeated videotaping during my sessions with her and review of her behavior during impromptu questioning helped her to break the habit. Once the laugh diminished, so did her foot tapping.

Impressive Appearance

Choices of clothing for presidential debaters have narrowed considerably. The navy suit with lapels less than 4 inches, a white shirt, and red tie seems to be the uniform of choice for men says Georges de Paris, a Washington tailor. Luckily, women have many more choices, but remember that our goal is to enhance our communication not to create a conversation about our outfit. Lillian Brown, a media coach, spent hours shopping for the fabulous blue dress worn by Ann Richards as she delivered the keynote address for the 1998 Democratic Convention in Atlanta. Lillian studied the background color of the podium, the lighting, the depth of camera coverage, and Ann's personal characteristics; her silver hair, her blue-green eyes and her vibrant personality before choosing the perfect dress. It is critical that we choose the correct clothing for an event so that we can be confident and comfortable. Once the clothing is chosen, we can focus on preparing for the performance.

I advise clients to have several presentation outfits that are not worn for any other occasion. Depending on your profession, a suit, jacket and skirt, jacket and pants, or sweater and pants may be appropriate. These outfits should fit well and be of a finer fabric and a color that flatters you. Skirts should be of a length that is most flattering to your legs and to your profession. Be sure to sit down and determine whether the skirt rises to an appropriate length. You want to be focused on the interaction, not on how much of your thigh is showing. The length of your pants should be appropriate for the height of the heel of your shoes and should barely touch the instep of your shoe. Stand before a three-way mirror in your selected attire and determine if the style, fit, and color is well-suited for the event. Remember, what you choose to wear and how you look can have a great effect on what others think of you and what you think of yourself.

When a client enters the office for executive training, dressed informally in shorts or jeans, even if it is her day off or casual Friday, I immediately question her seriousness. I don't expect a client to dress up for training, but her confidence during training will be greater if she is dressed suitably and comfortably. Your goal is to look the part whether you are lecturing to your colleagues, presenting a design to an advertising firm, selling pharmaceutical products, or interviewing for a new position. Remember, you are selling the entire package, not just your credentials.

It is far more practical to assemble several stunning, classic outfits than to strive for variety and purchase inexpensive trendy fashions. The same is true of accessories and hair style. You don't want to be continually adjusting a loose fitting scarf, bra strap, or piece of hair that flips over your eye at the most inopportune time. Your jewelry should accent and not distract from your presence. Perform a dress rehearsal wearing your chosen outfit and accessories several days prior to your big event. You are working against yourself the morning of the presentation if you are scrambling to find a belt or iron your blouse thirty minutes before you are to leave the house. Those critical last minutes should be spent gathering your materials, adjusting make-up, and being sure that your opening is set.

Impressive Appearance Pointers

- **Invest time and money in your executive presence.**
- **Determine your optimal style, color and fabric.**
- **Assemble several "presentation only" outfits.**
- **Perform a dress rehearsal prior to the event.**
- **Contact an image consultant or salesperson for help.**

If you have no idea of what clothing style, color, or fabric to buy, contact an image consultant or make an appointment with a sales person in the women's fashion department at a more expensive department store. You are not obligated to buy and will be able to see yourself in a variety of outfits chosen specifically for you. Be certain to bring a trusted friend along if you feel shy about being the center of attention. Developing an executive presence is hard work and requires risk, but it is one of the finest investments in time and money that you will ever make.

PLAYING YOUR VOCAL INSTRUMENT

"Nasal Nelda"

Many people I train believe we are born with an unal-terable, "given" voice. While it is true that physical size and body type dictate the length and mass of our vocal folds and the boundaries of our pitch, the resonance or overall tone of your voice depends on the openness of the pharynx or back of our throat, mouth and nose. Who doesn't pick actor James Earl Jones either first or second when thinking of voices that are most pleasing to the ear? Jones's deep, seductive, and resonant vocal tone is created by a very relaxed and open throat with room in the oral cavity to amplify the tone. I would guess that his vocal folds are not much longer or more massive than an average male's, but his ability to "play his vocal instrument" is phenomenal!

Contrast the nasal tones of Rosie O'Donnell or Joan Rivers with the soothing deeper tones of Maya Angelo or Christiane Amanpour. The differences lie in their use of breath, tenseness or laxity of vocal fold vibration, open or closed throat, relaxed or tight jaw, and precise or inaccurate articulation. Everyone can learn to play their vocal instrument and to vary their tone appropriately for the situation. I will use a softer, breathier tone in a quiet, intimate restaurant with my husband, but will speak with a louder and full, but lower-pitched voice in a larger corporate setting or professional speaking engagement. My soft, breathy voice would not be consistent with my professional image at a conference or client interview.

Let's see how you sound! Call your answering machine and leave yourself a message or tape record your voice on several different occasions. Play the messages back and analyze the vocal tone. Ask yourself the following questions:

- Is the pitch of your voice appropriate for your age and size?
- Does your vocal tone sound thin and nasal?
- Do you clench your jaw when concentrating?
- Is the volume of your voice too loud or too soft?
- Does your vocal range span two octaves?

▓ Do you attack vowels in an abrupt or breathy way?

▓ Does your throat feel tight when you are stressed?

If you don't have the time to call your answering machine and want to hear your real voice right now, do the following. Cup each hand into a half-moon with your palms facing forward and place each hand behind your ear. Your palms will continue to face forward. Now count to 10 or recite a poem that you know. Your voice will sound very different to you. The bad news is that this voice is the one that others hear when you speak to them. It is also the voice that you hear when you play back your recorded voice. But why does it sound so different to you?

Humans hear sounds through both air and bone conduction. Air conduction means that the air conducts sound into your pinna or outer ear. Then the sound is processed by your inner ear. Air conduction is how we hear other people's voices, environmental sounds, and music. Bone conduction means that sound vibrates in the bones of your skull. When you speak, you hear yourself through the bones of your skull, which makes your voice sound more resonant and full to you. When you cup your hands around your ears, you are allowing air conduction to override bone conduction so you hear yourself as others hear you, chiefly through sound waves coming into your ears and less through vibrations within your skull.

Your voice, like many of your behaviors, has been learned and is a habit. The good news is that you can change your voice quickly. Changing it requires good instruction and that you like the sound of the "new you."

Your Best Pitch

When Lori called to schedule an appointment, I assumed that she was an adolescent because her voice was high-pitched, breathy, and soft in volume. On the day of the appointment in walked a 32-year-old female attorney specializing in tax law for a large real estate company. Lori came for training because her voice sounded gravelly to her. She was concerned about periodic hoarseness as she was the lead for a female rock band and could no longer belt her high notes.

As her hoarseness and range improved, I tried valiantly to alter Lori's vocal image. I replayed several saved phone messages to her, attempting to convince her to lower her pitch. She and I compared the audio of her present thin-toned recordings with her new deeper, pleasant tone. She even asked for friends' honest opinions about the sound of her new voice, and they loved her new sound. Nevertheless, Lori completed training after several sessions and left speaking with a gravel-free, but still high-pitched, breathy, soft voice. I was hesitant to see her go because I knew that she was bored at work and wished for a more exciting legal position. I'm afraid voice will be an obstacle for her in her professional life.

On the other hand, meet Marion, one of the few female explosives experts in the world, who works for an agency of the Department of Defense. Marion came for help because she loved to sing, and a "warble" had appeared in her singing voice. Although Marion was trained classically and sang as a soprano, she spoke with effort, in a very restricted manner at the bottom of her pitch range. Her voice sounded tight, as if her "parking brake was on." With conscious attention to breathing and opening the back of her throat, Marion began to use her entire instrument in speaking. She learned to speak as she sings, allowing air to naturally produce her vocal tone. Her warble disappeared and no one at work even realized that her voice was different. Looking back, Marion was convinced that she had adapted the lower pitch to fit in with the Defense Department culture.

If you are speaking at too low or too high of a pitch, your voice can be effortful to produce. There are several tricks to finding out where your own "best pitch" resides. If you have a piano and can sing even close to key, start in the middle of your range and sing the vowel sounds *ee* or *oo* down the scale as far as you can go. If you don't have a piano, go to the website www.music.vt.edu/musicdictionary/pianopitch and use the keyboard. Don't worry if you are not musical. Make note of the lowest sound that you can sing, but don't include notes at the very bottom of your range where you sound like you are croaking. Then start in the middle of your range again and sing the vowel as high as you can go. Make note of your highest sound and whether it includes the "falsetto" or "Frankie Valli" register, a vibrating mode in which only the edges of the vocal fold approximate to produce a very high tone.

Grant Fairbanks, who established this procedure to find one's "optimal pitch," asked his singers to locate their lowest and highest pitches and then to proceed one-third of the way up the range if they didn't include falsetto and one-fourth of the way if they did use falsetto to find their "optimal pitch." This is easy to do. Mark your lowest note and your highest and then count how many whole notes there are in between. If your range included the very high or falsetto register, count one-fourth of the way up the range. If it didn't, count one-third of the way up the range. These notes identify a speaker's or singer's best speaking pitch. In training, I will mark this spot and then coach the client to speak two to three notes around the spot assuring that the sound is initiated with air from her lungs as in singing. Cup your palms around your ears and see if you like your new voice.

Another widely used formula for finding a speaker's "natural tone" was initiated by Morton Cooper. Cooper asks clients to say *um hum?* spontaneously to the question: Do you want a million dollars? The use of this starter focuses the voice upward and forward into the nose. I modify this method by asking clients to say *um hum?* or *meme*, followed by counting from 1 to 10; *meme* 1, *meme* 2, etc. The *meme*, like *um hum?*, focuses the sound in your nose while the numbers are focused in your mouth. Be sure to stretch out the vowels in the numbers so that they sound like a glide; *memeooone*, *memetwooo*, etc. I count to 10 using the *meme* as a starter every morning to warm up my voice. During a conversation, Cooper advocates saying *um hum?* when listening during a conversation so that the next comment you make will be appropriately pitched. This is easy to do and works like a charm.

If your voice sounds thin and breathy like Melanie Griffith's did in Working Girl, try speaking a bit lower in pitch while tapping your upper chest. The emitted sound should waver but be fuller because your sound is now generated from the lungs. It is the air from your lungs that produces the tone that you shape into words and sentences. When your voice is higher pitched and thin, typically, only your lips and mouth are talking without sound generated from your lungs.

Stand up and count from 1 to 10 as if you are telling a story so that your voice has inflection while still tapping your chest. Relax your throat and just let the sound come out. Say the days of the week or recite the Pledge of Allegiance as you tap your chest. Concentrate solely on air coming from your body producing the tone that your mouth shapes into words. Your vocal folds will remain loose, producing a lower-pitched sound, not high pitched and tight as if only your lips and mouth are talking. Soon eliminate the tapping and begin to feel the new sound generated within your chest.

Whether we call it your best, optimal, or natural pitch, I find that your vocal instrument works most efficiently when air from your lungs allows your relaxed vocal folds to produce tone effortlessly. When we speak down on our vocal folds, the tone sounds deep and gravelly. It may feel like your parking brake is on, prohibiting the air from flowing freely. Speaking at too high a pitch isn't good either. You are unable to speak louder, without squeaking, and you may sound much younger than you are.

Begin now to find your "best voice" each morning before you go to work.

- Tap your chest as you count from 1 to 10 to free up your sound.
- Recite *meme-oone, meme-twoo* up to *meme-teen* to focus your voice appropriately.
- Insert *meme* at the beginning as you recite a poem you know.
- Your goal is to allow your vocal folds to vibrate naturally producing a tone that resounds within your body.
- You may sound weird at first, but I promise you that an energetic, relaxed voice will emerge to replace your croaky morning voice.

Your Best Pitch Pointers

- *Calculate your "best pitch."*
- **Use um hum? or meme to focus your voice properly every morning.**
- *Generate tone with air from your lungs.*
- *Don't drop into gravel at the end of your sentence.*
- **Say um hum? out loud when listening during a conversation.**

Resonant Voice Quality

Say an **M** or **N** sound and place your finger lightly on the side of your nose. Do you feel vibration? You should! Now, pinch your nostrils shut and say an **M** or an **N** sound. You can't produce these sounds with your nose closed off. **M**, **N**, and **NG** sounds (for example, sing) are called nasal tones because the uvula or end of your soft palate stays down, allowing air to go into your nose when you say these sounds (see Illustration 1). All other sounds, such as **S**, **Z**, **T**, **D**, **R**, etc., resonate within the mouth because the soft palate raises to close off the nose, and the sound can only come through the mouth (see Illustration 2).

**ILLUSTRATION 1 –
SOUND COMES OUT THE
NASAL CAVITY**

**ILLUSTRATION 2 –
SOUND COMES OUT THE
ORAL CAVITY**

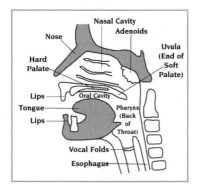

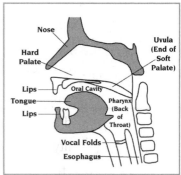

Only nasal tones should resonate within your nose or nasal cavity. If you have a cold and your nose is stopped up, a hollow, dull, non-nasal tone results. Sound cannot resonate in your nose and **Ms** and **Ns** sound more like **Ps** and **Bs**. This muffled voice is the opposite of the more common irritating nasal tone where sounds other than **Ms**, **Ns** or **NGs** resonate in the nose. Comedians frequently use this munchkin or nasal Minnie Mouse sound which is entertaining in small doses, but is annoying in real life. Either too much or too little nasality can immensely affect your image.

Bill Bradley's dull, hollow voice may have negatively affected his chance for the Democratic candidacy in the 2000 Presidential election primaries. Most likely, a deviated septum from injuries sustained during years of playing basketball resulted in blocked nasal passages and his dull, non-resonant voice. He was a Rhodes Scholar with stellar ideas, but his vocal tone lacked the energy, clarity, and enthusiasm essential for a Presidential candidate. An extremely nasal voice can be even worse. Nelda called and left a message. She was a radio reporter who had moved to Washington, D.C. from Chicago and could not find a job. I returned her call praying that she despised the nasality of her voice as much as I hated hearing it. As Nelda learned to relax her jaw and tongue and resonate the vowels within her mouth and not her nose, a deeper, pleasant tone emerged. She was soon hired by National Public Radio and loves her work and social life in D.C.

When you listened to your answering machine message, did you detect even slight nasality in your voice? If so, it may be very easy to change. A nasal voice quality frequently occurs when there is not enough space for vowels and non-nasal sounds such as L, R, Y, V, G, Z, V, etc., to resonate in the mouth, so they resonate in the nose. Be brave. Stand in front of a mirror and watch your mouth movement as you count from 1 to 15. Is there some space between your upper and lower teeth as you talk? Does your bottom jaw lower slightly for vowels such as *a* (*aw*) or *o* (*oh*)? Recite a familiar poem and watch to see if your jaw remains more clenched or more open.

Nasal speakers tend to clench their jaws when they are tense and often report teeth gritting at night. Be a detective and observe whether this happens to you, especially when you are under pressure. Become aware when you tighten your jaw and consciously release those muscles. Try to keep your molars or back teeth slightly apart during the day when you are not speaking. Relax your jaw and allow it to move freely as you speak. These two tips may eliminate your nasal sound. Place a small mirror by your telephone to remind you to maintain a longer face and looser jaw as you speak.

If relaxing your jaw does not significantly alter your nasality, practice saying the following sentences. These sentences contain no nasal sounds, so you should concentrate on forming the vowel sounds. The vowels are underlined to assist you in emphasizing them:

NON-NASAL SENTENCES

- Pete eats peas with leeks.
- Tod sought to stop the cop.
- The five blue jewels are sold.
- Who told Joel about the oil?

Now, say each sentence in a very nasal way almost scrunching up your nose to do so, and then produce it correctly with a relaxed jaw and well-formed non-nasal vowels. Negative practice or practicing the wrong way and then the new way is very difficult but will help you to master your new voice more quickly. Cupping your hands around your ears as was discussed in the beginning of this chapter also will provide you excellent auditory feedback as to how you really sound. Once you can produce vowels without sounding nasal, move on to the next set of sentences. This practice set is loaded with the nasal sounds *M*, *N*, and *NG*, which will be much more difficult for you.

NASAL SENTENCES

- Many men make money in marketing telecommunication.
- My mother Martha Mary Miller may munch on mackerel and macaroni.
- The marvelous musicians sang nineteen stanzas of Mozart.

The trick now is to allow the *M*, *N*, and *NG* sounds to resonate through the nose while the other sounds resonate through the mouth. It is important to concentrate on relaxing your lower jaw in pronouncing these sentences. As a challenge, use negative practice again to scrunch up your nose and sound horribly nasal at first on all of the words. Then practice sounding nasal for all of the *M*, *N*, and *NG* sounds, but not for the vowels and non-nasal consonants. This may be difficult, but I guarantee you that daily practice on these two groups of sentences will help you greatly.

If you sound hollow and dull with no or little nasal resonance on the nasal sounds, you'll need to emphasize the nasality of the *M*, *N*, and *NG* sounds. First, let's see if your nose is working properly. Cover one nostril with your index finger and exhale to see if any air can flow from that nostril.

Then cover the opposite nostril and exhale again. If only a minimal amount of air can flow from either nostril as you exhale, please consult an otolaryngologist or ear, nose, and throat doctor for help. It is impossible to attain proper nasality for *M*, *N* or *NG* sounds when no air can enter or leave the nose.

If you find that air does flow from each nostril, then practice the *M*, *N* and *NG* sentences again, but this time be certain to exaggerate or prolong the nasal sounds. Practice these and other sentences on a daily basis until you are able to make the needed transition between the *M*, *N*, and *NG* sounds which resonate in the nose and the vowels which resonate in the mouth. Learning a new behavior takes daily practice but the reward is well worth your effort.

Resonant Voice Quality Pointers

- *Maintain space between your teeth as you speak.*
- *Keep your molars slightly apart during the day.*
- *Form your vowel sounds.*
- *Resonate M, N, and NG properly.*
- *Move your lower jaw smoothly as you speak.*

Appropriate Loudness

"You've spoken at the top of your lungs as long as I can remember," Ellen's mom told Ellen during the initial consultation. "When you talk to me on your cell phone, I have to hold the phone at least an arm's length away."

Ellen was entering her senior year at the University of Virginia and planned to attend law school the following year. Within the confines of my office, her voice was excessively loud; and I could only imagine how loudly she spoke in a bustling, noisy restaurant. After we determined that her hearing was normal, it was time to train Ellen's ears: first, to actually hear the loudness of her voice, and second, to calibrate the volume of her voice in differing environments. Training centered primarily on teaching her to coordinate the driving force of her breath with the openness of her throat in very quiet and in very loud settings. As Ellen transitioned use of her "new voice" into social interactions, she noticed that strangers were responsive to her and did not back away from her when she spoke. Mom was thrilled that Ellen no longer "screamed" into the phone.

Extroverted, energetic, and people-oriented women in occupations such as advertising, sales, media, and marketing may speak with more intensity and drive than women in such professions as medicine, law, finance, or research. Certainly most of us speak louder when we are really angry or threatened. Vocal intensity is learned and habituated at a young age and appears dependent on the number, birth order and ages of the speaker's siblings, home noise level, interests and personality profile. Adolescent girls actively involved in sports, theater, chorus and cheerleading frequently experience hoarseness and loss of voice from overusing their voices. These performers share similar personality and vocal traits that will continue into adulthood unless they learn to play their vocal instrument efficiently and effectively early in life.

It is hard to gauge the volume of your own voice. If you are born with an instrument like James Earl Jones that resonates well, you may find yourself speaking much louder than you need to and be totally unaware of it. Sometimes it becomes necessary for a friend or family member to inconspicuously tape record your voice and hand you the tape. I frequently suggest that new clients place a small digital recorder in their pockets or purses and tape their conversations in a multitude of situations. If you find that your voice is inappropriately loud, lower your volume. This does not mean modifying your personality and becoming a shy introvert compared to your bubbly, energetic self. It simply involves adjusting the amount of air you inhale and learning to maintain it within your lower thorax or rib cage and replenish it as needed when talking. Ask a trusted friend to signal you when you speak more loudly than you need to.

Many women report that they cannot project their voices and cannot be heard, the first time or anytime. Monica worked in a think tank for public policy issues. At thirty-five and as the only female candidate, she was vying for second in command of a large, highly respected firm. Although her ideas were brilliant and logically presented, she frequently felt sidestepped during weekly briefings. I used a 1-5 scale in the following acoustic settings to measure the volume of her voice:

1. Speaking very quietly in a movie theater
2. Conducting a one-to-one conversation in a small office
3. Speaking to six colleagues in a conference room
4. Projecting in a loud restaurant
5. Speaking loudly during a rock concert,

Monica spoke at a 1.5 level during our initial meeting in my small office. As we explored speaking with more volume, Monica felt that she was yelling, which offended her.

Monica was a very intelligent, accomplished academic with insight and passion for the big picture, yet her views frequently were not heard because the volume of her voice was so low. She agreed that her very soft voice diminished her effectiveness and was willing to recalibrate her internal loudness meter. In the office, Monica quickly learned to use her lower thorax and abdomen for better breath support. She could readily adapt to speaking louder or softer within the office, but had great difficulty transferring her intensity changes to outside settings. Much of our training involved Monica's learning which volume setting was appropriate for different environments. As we entered differing acoustic settings, she would signal me with the volume number that she perceived as correct, then would speak at that volume. Within days, she had recalibrated her feedback system, and could monitor her intensity well; however, this required painstaking conscious attention at first.

Begin now to listen critically to your volume fluctuations and determine if your levels match those of other speakers. If you speak too softly, learning to speak louder will not require a personality makeover, just as in decreasing your intensity will not catapult you into social withdrawal. Once you can monitor your loudness appropriately, the motoric

- **Listen critically to your volume fluctuations.**

- **Compare your speaking intensity level to other speakers.**

- **Learn to calibrate your vocal intensity.**

- **Aim for an intensity level of 2 to 2.5 on my volume scale.**

- **Learn the mechanics of breath control in chapter 3.**

aspects of breath control for speaking are easy to learn. For softer intensity phonation or sound, a smaller amount of air is initially inhaled and replenished when needed. Speaking louder requires a larger amount of inhaled air initially and greater thoracic muscle control to support your breath throughout the utterance. Turn to chapter 3 now, if you are ready to learn these adjustments.

Extensive Vocal Range

Whether you can carry a tune or not, your vocal folds should be able to vibrate over a two octave range. Just as you stretch your leg muscles and ligaments before you walk or run, you need to keep your vocal muscles exercised and toned. Your vocal folds are comprised of muscles and ligaments that behave similarly to your other muscles. They lose mass and tone with age and disuse. If the mass and elasticity of the vocal folds lessens, they may bow and be unable to approximate each other adequately enough to vibrate throughout the entire utterance. This is why women as young as sixty often report difficulty projecting their voices and become raspy or whispery.

Interestingly, trained singers who speak below their "best" pitch for most of the day frequently report that they can no longer reach their high notes. Remember Monica, the explosives expert, who acquired a lower pitch to fit in with the guys at the Defense Department. Her singing voice at the lower pitches began to warble or tremble and she could no longer reach her high soprano notes. Untrained singers and speakers such as Monica who speak at too low or too high a pitch frequently discover that their vocal range is greatly decreased and that more effort is necessary to speak louder in noisy environments.

These women especially, but all women in general, would benefit from a daily vocal exercise routine geared toward adding bulk to their vocal folds and flexibility to the vocal muscles and ligaments. Begin the following program immediately and record your results.

(SAMPLE)

GOALS: TO IMPROVE VOCAL FOLD VIBRATION AND EXTEND VOCAL RANGE

Baseline: (Sept. 27, 2005)   Sustained **ee** or **oo**: 15 seconds

Lowest note: A2 Highest note: C4

EXERCISE	REPS	28-Sep	29-Sep	30-Sep	01-Oct	02-Oct	03-Oct	04-Oct	05-Oct	06-Oct	07-Oct	08-Oct
Sustain ee or oo sound	2	X	X	X	X	X	X	X	X	X	X	X
Glide from low to high pitch	2	X	X	X	X	X	X	X	X	X	X	X
Glide from high to low pitch	2	X	X	X	X	X	X	X	X	X	X	X
Lip flutter with sound	2	X	X	X	X	X	X	X	X	X	X	X
Lip flutter low to high pitch	2	X	X	X	X	X	X	X	X	X	X	X
Lip flutter high to low pitch	2	X	X	X	X	X	X	X	X	X	X	X

Use the blank exercise chart below to track your progress.

GOALS: TO IMPROVE VOCAL FOLD VIBRATION AND EXTEND VOCAL RANGE

Baseline: (date:)   Sustained **ee** or **oo**: 15 seconds

Lowest note: Highest note:

EXERCISE	REPS	DATE								
Sustain ee or oo sound	2									
Glide from low to high pitch	2									
Glide from high to low pitch	2									
Lip flutter with sound	2									
Lip flutter low to high pitch	2									
Lip flutter high to low pitch	2									

*PLEASE NOTE: enlargements of charts are on pages 194 and 195.

Voice Exercise Program

First you must obtain two baseline vocal assessments so that you can measure your progress. Record them on your chart.

ESTABLISH YOUR BASELINE

- Say the vowel *e* (*ee*) or *u* (*oo*) at a comfortable pitch for as long as you can without pushing or strain. Do this three times and note your best time.

- Sing the vowel *e* (*ee*) or *u* (*oo*) down a scale as far as you can go and then as high as you can go. Do this three times and record your lowest note and your highest note.

- If you have already found your highest and lowest notes on the piano when determining your best pitch, note them. If you don't have a piano, go to the website www.music.vt.edu/musicdictionary/pianopitch and use the keyboard. Don't worry if you can't sing or sound flat. Just sing the vowel down as low as you can and then up as high as you can. Record the note that most closely matches your lowest and highest sound.

Now the fun begins! These exercises require patience at first, but they are fun to do and you will see improvement quickly. The routine will take two to three minutes every day.

DAILY ROUTINE

1. When you wake up in the morning or at night, sustain the vowel *e* (*ee*) or *u* (*oo*) at a comfortable pitch level and softly for as long as you can. Do this two times. Your goal is to hold this note for a long time, but don't push or strain to maintain the sound.

2. Glide or slide like a siren on the vowel *e* (*ee*) or *u* (*oo*) from as low to as high as you can go two times in a row. Be sure to allow time in between attempts to inhale sufficient breath. Now glide from as high as you can go to as low as you can go. Do this two times.

DAILY ROUTINE (CONT.)

3. Perform a lip flutter, which sounds similar to the motor-boat sound you made as a kid, or a tongue trill that you learned in Spanish, French or Italian class for as long as you can. Lip flutter or tongue trill at whatever pitch is most comfortable for you. Do this two times.

    a. Many of you physically cannot perform a tongue trill so don't worry about it. Work on the lip flutter. If you can't get your lips to flutter at first, stand up to drive more air through your vocal folds. Some clients find it easier to perform a lip flutter if they push each side of their lips closer together with their index fingers.

    b. If you still cannot do a flutter, perform a raspberry, which is the same as a lip flutter except you place your tongue between your lips and push out air from your lungs.

    c. Lip flutters, raspberries and tongue trills have little to do with your lips and tongue and everything to do with the driving force of your breath.

4. Perform a lip flutter or tongue trill slide or glide from your lowest note to your highest note and then take a breath and glide back down. Do this two times.

   a. You can glide up or down the scale in one slow but continuous sliding movement or proceed up or down note by note.

   b. The range of your lip flutter or tongue trill glide may be about three to four notes larger than your range when using vowels.

5. Every week, time the number of seconds that you can sustain your most comfortable sound and reassess your range. Time both vowels and flutters to see which sound yields better results. As you become more proficient at sustaining sounds and performing glides, do each exercise only one time.

NOTE: Lip flutters and tongue trills are optimal drills, if you can perform them, because they require optimal coordination of breath and vocal fold vibration with no vocal strain. The goal is to exert less respiratory effort or breath to achieve the same vibratory result over time.

Smooth Voice Onsets

Do you tend to interrupt others and speak quickly?

Listen closer and note whether you also initiate vowels very abruptly or loudly. An abrupt onset on a word such as *I* occurs when the speaker initiates sound by forcefully holding the vocal folds together then sharply releasing them. This way of speaking is abusive to the vocal folds, but even worse, can signal an offensive, impatient or demanding personality.

Extensive Vocal Range Pointers

■ *Obtain your baseline range.*

■ *Sustain your most comfortable sound for as long as possible once a day.*

■ *Practice lip flutters, raspberries, or tongue trill glides once a day.*

■ *Measure your progress weekly at first.*

■ *Lip flutter when driving in rush hour traffic.*

The opposite is true when you initiate speech in a tentative, breathy, delicate manner, which happens when the vocal folds don't close sufficiently and excessive air accompanies the sound. A whispery onset is appropriate for an intimate setting with your husband or boyfriend, but unacceptable in a boardroom.

I realize that you have never even thought about this! Listen to the message on your answering machine and analyze whether you sound like Betsy or Alicia.

"I grew up in Upstate New York, in a city called Ithaca."

Betsy was a coxswain for her university crew team and developed vocal nodules on both of her vocal folds. Nodules are similar to calluses that form on your toe from ill-fitting shoes. Nodules frequently occur one-third of the way along both vocal folds, the place where they vibrate maximally. Teenagers and adult women may develop these from initiating the voice too abruptly or closing the vocal folds too forcefully when speaking. Nodules can occur also in weight lifters or tennis players who grunt as they lift or serve a tennis ball. Betsy's nodules were caused by her sharp vocal onsets when talking and further compounded by shouting commands during crew practice. Betsy's nodules resolved within six weeks of voice training, as she modified her aggressive vocal style and learned to project commands properly. She maintained her Type A personality, but learning to breathe while listening greatly diminished her tendency to interrupt others.

Alicia wished to present herself more diplomatically at the embassy. Although well educated and with perfect credentials for her highly ranked position, she was never called upon to share her opinions. Alicia initiated her speech with an extremely breathy sound and very soft intensity, almost sounding like an *H* sound preceded every vowel. She rapidly ran out of air and gasped to get more in when she spoke fervently about a topic. Alicia had a Marilyn Monroe or Jackie Kennedy sounding voice. In training, she learned how to initiate speech more briskly using only minimal air and good vocal fold closure. She practiced her assigned lists of words incessantly and developed vocal power by learning to maintain her breath through the end of her sentences.

Smooth Voice Onset Pointers

■ *Take a small breath before you speak.*

■ *If vowel starts are abrupt, extend the vowel.*

■ *If vowel onsets are breathy, initiate vowels crisply.*

■ *Converse in a legato or smoothly connected manner.*

When we wish to produce sound, our vocal folds meet as air from the lungs flows through the vocal folds sucking them together initially then repetitively opening and closing them to produce sound until breath is replenished. Vowels should be produced not sharply or weakly but smoothly with well-timed vocal fold closure and coordinated airflow.

If you produce vowels like Betsy or Alicia continue to read this section. If you don't, proceed to chapter 3.

If you produce your first vowel too abruptly, like Betsy, the coxswain, read the following sentences and initiate the vowels smoothly. Try to imagine that two vowels exist so that the vowel is slightly prolonged. Practice reading the words in Column 1. Be sure to take a small breath before you speak. If prolonging the vowel does not work for you, think of saying a small *H* sound before the vowel. Practice Column 2. Both techniques will help you to initiate vowels less sharply.

Column 1	Column 2
egg (imagine *eegg*)	*h*egg
Annie (imagine AAnie)	*h*Annie
institution (imagine *ii*nstitution)	*h*institution
I **o**rdered **a**n **o**melette	*h*I *h*ordered *h*an *h*omelette.
(**II** *oor*dered **aan** **oo**melette.)	

If you tend to hit words starting with vowels too aggressively, try to smoothly connect your words within sentences, practicing with the sentences below. Your speech should sound less abrupt and choppy.

VOWEL SENTENCES

▧ I am excited about our outing in the Appalachian outdoors.

▧ Albert eats hundreds of eggs every afternoon at about one o'clock.

▧ Uncle Eddie invented eleven incredible islands out of icicles.

▧ I am ordering an omelette with onions, artichokes, and anchovies.

COMPETENCY 3

Mastering Breath Control

"Timid Tina"

"I can't stop shaking, both internally and externally," shrieked Tina. Other physical symptoms of performance anxiety or "stage fright" may include increased heart rate, sweaty palms, runny nose, shortness of breath, shakiness, upset stomach, inability to think clearly, vocal tremor, or excessive perspiration. Speaking from experience, I know to bring a tissue for my runny nose and to bite my tongue to increase saliva immediately prior to a lecture. These symptoms signal me that my adrenalin is working and that I am physiologically ready for action. Then I initiate and maintain a very slow rhythmical pattern of breathing which informs my body that all is well and I am in no physical danger.

Once you understand your autonomic nervous system and welcome your specific arousal signals, you can decrease them with a few simple tricks and control of your breathing. "Timid Tina" would begin to shake, clear her throat and feel her chest tighten three speakers before her turn to introduce herself to prospective clients seated around the conference table. When her turn came, her voice would be soft in intensity and squeaky. Once she learned to breathe with an open throat and relaxed vocal folds, her shakiness subsided and she gained confidence in her ability to speak with certainty. Viewing herself on video helped to convince Tina that her internal turmoil was not observable to others.

Gaining conscious control of our breathing as taught in Lamaze classes and yoga enables us to handle many difficult situations. Pay attention to your body and your breathing patterns when you become tense or uptight. Discover whether any of the following are true of you:

■ Do you hold your breath as you rush to your meeting a few minutes late?

■ Do your shoulders, neck and chest muscles tighten before or while you are speaking?

- Does your upper chest rise when you inhale air prior to speaking?
- Do you speak quickly, almost gasping for breath between thoughts?
- Do the ends of your sentences trail off as you are speaking?
- Can you project your voice easily in a noisy restaurant?

The exercises that follow will help you to learn relaxed breathing, when to replenish your breaths when speaking, and how to breathe to project your voice. These exercises may appear complicated and time consuming, but please read and practice them at least once. Understanding the spontaneity of your breathing will allow you to remain calm under pressure. Gaining control of your breathing will permit you to project your voice with decreased effort.

RELAXED NON-SPEECH BREATHING

Try this. Breathe through your nose and relax your lower jaw. Your molars will be slightly apart and your face will be longer. Now with your lips closed, place your tongue tip lightly behind your upper front teeth or lightly below your bottom front teeth. This will open up the back of your throat and allow the perfect amount of air to flow easily into your lower lungs and back out. Perform this cycle three or four times in a row allowing air to spontaneously flow in both directions. You may note that only a small amount of air goes in and out. That is good. You want gravity to allow the flow of air — not you filling up your chest with air and then pushing it all out. Mastery of this relaxed pattern of breathing will require conscious attention at first, but it will enable you to remain calm as the world bustles around you.

I ask clients to use this pattern of breathing as they walk to their cars in the morning or enter their office buildings. Don't wait until you are late for an office briefing to use relaxed breathing. Start relaxed breathing as you look at the clock, realize that you are late and jump up from your chair. Once in the conference room and seated, consciously key in again to your breath, because I guarantee that you are holding your breath wondering what you have missed. Try to use this pattern of breathing at least three times per day when you are not stressed. Use it as you drive to work, when you are reading your e-mail and when you are walking to the water cooler.

Relaxed Non-Speech Breathing Pointers

- **Breathe through your nose.**

- **Keep your molars slightly apart with your lips closed.**

- **Place your tongue tip lightly behind your upper or lower front teeth.**

- **The perfect amount of air will come in.**

I promise you that a week of conscious attention to "relaxed breathing" will quiet your body and allow you to focus on the high-priority issues at hand. Put a penny in your pocket three days in a row. When you feel the penny, instantly relax your lower jaw and breathe in a conscious relaxed way for three cycles of inhalation and exhalation. Once this pattern becomes automatic when walking or listening to someone on the phone, begin to access it during more challenging interactions.

Coordinated Speech Breathing

Katie was a classically trained opera singer who worked for the Defense Department by day and sang as an amateur with the National Cathedral Choir several evenings per week. Although Katie well understood how and when to breathe when singing, she spoke very quickly and with run-on sentences containing three to four thoughts. She audibly gasped to inhale air quickly in between her long sentences, appearing as if she might "lose the floor" if she slowed down to take a breath. Unfortunately, I could hardly remember all of the points that Katie presented. Contrast Katie's delivery with a speaker who delivers a clear message, speaking slowly and pausing appropriately to replenish her breath. Do you ever find yourself breathing like Katie?

Before you can even learn when to breathe, you must first determine how much breath you have! Here are some exercises to help you evaluate your breathing.

CURRENT BREATHING LEVEL

1. Take a deep breath and then as you exhale, sustain an *S* sound for as long as you can. It will sound like a soft hiss. You should be able to hold this sound for at least 15 seconds.

If you can't sustain your breath for at least 15 seconds, stand up and try again. Since breath is the driving force which keeps your vocal folds vibrating, if you only have 8 to 10 seconds of air, you will not be able, physically, to project your voice. If you are short of breath, please see your internist or your pulmonologist for further evaluation of your lung function. If you are a scuba diver or a saxophonist, you may be able to sustain an *S* for as long as a minute.

CURRENT BREATHING LEVEL (CONT.)

2. Take a deep breath and sustain a *Z* sound for as long as you can.

You should be able to hold your *Z* sound for about as long as your *S* sound. The length of the *S* sound provides an indirect measure of your lung volume, while length of the *Z* implies that your vocal folds are meeting sufficiently to vibrate throughout your entire exhalation. If you are one who can sustain an *S* forever, your *Z* will be longer than 18 seconds, but most likely won't equal your *S*. If your *S* sound lasts 18 seconds or longer and your *Z* sound lasts only 10 seconds or less, please consult your otolaryngologist or ear, nose and throat doctor to examine your vocal folds. Vocal fold problems such as weakness, vocal fold swellings, or a growth can prevent vocal folds from vibrating throughout the entire exhalation.

Now let's discover when and how you replenish your breath as you speak! The key to speaking effortlessly is knowing when and how to refill the air that you have used.

REPLENISHING YOUR BREATH WHEN SPEAKING

1. Take a breath and count from 1 to as far as you can on one breath. Note how your voice sounds and your throat feels as you run out of air? Do you begin to strain as you push out the last few numbers?

2. Take a smaller breath in and count by 10s increasing your loudness on the numbers 10, 20, 30, 40, and 50. It will look like this:

(small inhalation) 1 2 3 4 5 6 7 8 9 **10** (air comes in)
11 12 13 14 15 16 17 18 19 **20** (air comes in)
21 22 23 24 25 26 27 28 29 **30** (air comes in)
31 32 33 34 35 36 37 38 39 **40** (air comes in)
41 42 43 44 45 46 47 48 49 **50** (air comes in).

At the number 10, you probably weren't ready for air to come in, but as you counted higher, hopefully, you felt air coming in more naturally after **20**, **30**, **40** and **50**. Repeat this until you feel air naturally replenishing itself.

REPLENISHING YOUR BREATH
WHEN SPEAKING (CONT.)

3. If you are having a hard time feeling this, sing a song and note how easily the air comes in and how air is maintained through the end of the stanza before the next breath automatically occurs. Then speak the words to the song and replenish your breaths as you need to.

4. Take a small breath at the start and recite the days of the week over and over, pausing to breathe when you need to. Recite the months of the year in same way. You will take replenishing breaths more frequently when speaking more softly than when you are speaking more loudly. This happens because the vocal folds don't approximate or meet as firmly when we speak softly and a slight amount of air is released as you speak. Recite the months of the year loudly and see if this is true.

5. Read a paragraph from the newspaper aloud. First read the paragraph silently and mark a slash (/) where you think you will breathe. As you read the paper aloud, discover whether you took a breath where you thought you would or not. It doesn't matter as long as you are not running out of air as you speak.

There are two keys to breathing for speech. One is taking a smaller inhalation at the start of your utterance since inhaling too deeply can make you tense. The second is pausing when you need to, allowing the right amount of air to come in. Your brain will begin to coordinate your breathing with the length of what you plan to say. You will not find yourself taking a breath in the mid(inhale)dle of a word. Jeffrey Jacobi in How to Say It with Your Voice writes that we really are like a yellow rubber duck bath toy. When you squeeze the toy, air is forced out. When the pressure is released, the duck again sucks up the air it needs to regain its shape. Our breathing is similar: all you need to do is replace the air you breathe out. Breathe out, then replace. A natural intake of air will help you to effortlessly produce sound. It's that simple!

Coordinated Speech Breathing Pointers

- **Measure how long you can sustain S and Z.**

- **Don't take a huge inhalation before you start to speak.**

- **Allow replenishing breaths to occur naturally as you speak.**

- **Maintain your breath through the end of your thought.**

- **Slow down your speaking rate, if your inhalations are audible.**

Eased Vocal Projection

"I feel like a vice is tightening around my neck as I speak," strained Christine. Christine was an elementary school teacher who had just completed her first year of teaching first grade. She loved to teach but by November her voice sounded hoarse every evening. Time off for the Thanksgiving and Christmas vacations improved the raspiness of her voice, but by February, it was worse than ever and by 1 PM she needed to force out her voice to be heard by the students. Her neck and throat ached each evening and she winced in pain as she talked. I could hardly touch Christine's neck without her jerking away.

We discovered that Christine was using too much muscle to speak. Rather than using air to vibrate her vocal folds, she was pushing out sound with her false vocal folds, which are located right above your vocal folds. The false vocal folds serve a protective function for us when we swallow or lift something heavy but should not be used for speech. Basically, Christine was speaking with "her parking brake on."

The louder she needed to talk, the tighter the brake and the squeakier her sound. Immediately, Christine was willing to use a portable voice amplifier in her classroom, so that she could project her voice easily without strain. In training, she learned to release her parking brake (false vocal folds) and allow her lungs to work as a gas pedal to control her breath. Soon she was able to project her voice without the vocal amplifier. Christine also scheduled four "vocal breaks" during the day when the children worked quietly on written tasks.

First, let's review how to breathe correctly so you will be able to project your voice easily. Here are some exercises to help you project your voice.

PROJECT YOUR VOICE

1. Lie down on a bed or floor and exhale air as if you are gently blowing a feather. Let air come in naturally. You don't need to suck it in. Place your hand on your lower rib cage and breathe easily feeling the natural rise and fall of your lower rib cage. The perfect amount of air will come in. You may want to place a book on your stomach so that you can see the rise of your rib cage and abdomen during inhalation and the fall during exhalation. The good thing about lying down is that your shoulders can't rise up around your chin; and air will go into and out of your lower rib cage automatically.

Clients often ask why their abdomen expands during inhalation if air goes into the lower rib cage. Your diaphragm is a sheath that fits along the contour of your lower lungs. As your lungs expand the sheath enlarges just as when you blow air into a balloon the bottom of the balloon expands. When we exhale, as air comes out of the lungs, the sheath collapses adhering to the lower boundary of your rib cage.

PROJECT YOUR VOICE (CONT.)

2. Now stand up tall with your back against a door or wall. Be certain that your shoulders and head touch the door. Breathe easily and feel air coming into your lower rib cage during inhalation and leaving during exhalation. Don't try to suck in as much air as you can which will cause your upper chest to rise. Allow the right amount of air to come in naturally. It will, if you relax and let it happen.

3. Either lying down or standing against the door, produce a louder hiss or sustained **S** sound. Your lower rib cage should remain firmer and not collapse until you finish the sound. Now, do a series of long **S**s, slightly louder, with a pause in between. Be sure that your lower rib cage stays out for the sound then comes in when you pause before saying the next sound. The more forceful you make the **S** sound, the more rib cage movement you will feel.

S——— S——— - S——— S——— - S——— - S———

PROJECT YOUR VOICE (CONT.)

4. Standing against the wall, count from 1 to 50 as you did earlier in this chapter. But this time, concentrate on being sure that your ribcage stays out for the most part as you count. You will feel the loss of some air that will be replaced when you pause to allow air to come in. Pause at **10, 20** and **30** to replenish air. Remember to say the **10, 20** and **30** loudly so that your volume does not diminish at the end.

(small inhalation) 1 2 3 4 5 6 7 8 9 **10** (air comes in)
11 12 13 14 15 16 17 18 19 **20** (air comes in)
21 22 23 24 25 26 27 28 29 **30** (air comes in)

PROJECT YOUR VOICE (CONT.)

5. Finally, you are ready to speak louder. Now that you know how to use your air, you must form the words as if your mouth was a megaphone.

The trick is to relax your jaw and prolong the vowels slightly. Since vowels are the sounds that resonate and consonants simply add meaning, the vowels will carry your voice. To prove this point try to project a *T* or a *CH* sound. You hear a release of air only. Project an *AH* sound and hear the difference.

Say the following phrases loudly. Use a relaxed, deeper breath at the start and keep your throat relaxed. Exaggerate or stretch the vowel sounds. Cup your hands around your ears and listen to how loud you sound. You will be surprised!

MOVE OVER	(Mo-ove o-ove-er)
WATCH OUT	(Wa-atch ou-ut)
GO TEAM	(Go-o tea-am)

PROJECT YOUR VOICE (CONT.)

6. Read the first lines of the "Gettysburg Address" below. Vary your loudness.

Stand and pretend that you are reading it to six fellow workers in the conference room and then 20, then 100. The louder you need to speak, the more breath you will require at the start and the more you will need to stretch the vowels. This format for the "Gettysburg Address" is a bit different, so that you will breathe when you need to and not where punctuation tells you to. When projecting your voice to a crowd of 100 people, you should need a breath after the first line, since you will be speaking slowly to exaggerate the vowels.

Fourscore and seven years ago

our fathers brought forth on this continent

a new nation

conceived in liberty and dedicated to the proposition

that all men are created equal.

PROJECT YOUR VOICE (CONT.)

7. Practice varying the volume of your voice. Turn the radio on and converse pretending you are in a noisy restaurant. Be sure to use breath from your lower rib cage. Relax your throat, and speak more slowly so that your vowels are longer. If you start to feel vocal strain, place your hand on your lower ribcage to be sure that it is moving. Practice, so that you don't end up like the young woman in the following anecdote!

Eased Vocal Projection Pointers

- **Learn to breathe from your lower rib cage.**
- **Don't allow your rib cage to collapse as you speak.**
- **Prolong the vowels to achieve greater projection.**
- **Relax your jaw and throat when you speak loudly.**
- **Wear one foam ear plug in noisy environments.**

Susan, a twenty-year-old senior majoring in marketing, was ready to apply for her internship. The problem was that she usually lost her voice over the weekend and, frequently, could not speak above a whisper on Monday. The day Susan entered the clinic her voice was raspy, loud, and forced. I could see her neck muscles popping out as she spoke. Susan could tell that she spoke too loudly by the looks on people's faces when she spoke. She was tired of being the center of attention and wanted to learn to speak more professionally. Susan quickly learned to monitor the loudness of her voice and learned to vary her breath support when she spoke more quietly in class and on the phone and more loudly in busy restaurants. Susan was thrilled when she didn't lose her voice after a fun Saturday night. She also started drinking water and beer rather than whiskey and diet coke, limiting the alcohol and caffeine that dehydrated her vocal instrument. Susan also found that wearing one foam ear plug into noisy environments helped her to hear and feel when she strained or pushed out her voice. Susan was much better able to monitor her loudness. Drinking water also counteracted the drying effects of the beer.

Suitable Amplification

I advise clients to use a microphone if they are lecturing to a group of thirty or more people for longer than 20 minutes. If you practice the exercises listed above, you will be able to present to as many as 100 people without a microphone for an hour or so, but a microphone is helpful. Some speakers find that voice amplification via a microphone and public address system has a remarkable calming effect. Hearing their voices resonate through a good sound system coupled with their ability to project without effort creates a "positive feedback loop." These speakers literally "love to hear their voice" and finding the podium equipped with a functioning microphone is often all they need to feel confident and assured.

Suitable Amplification Pointers

- **Use a microphone if speaking to a large group for over 20 minutes.**

- **Arrive an hour early to check the facility.**

- **Keep the microphone an outstretched hand's width away from your chin.**

- **Rehearse your introduction.**

- **Confirm your loudness level.**

If you are not one of these fortunate folks, you will need to pay more attention to your breath control, your delivery rate and the effective use of pausing. Always arrive at least one hour before a key speaking engagement to locate the room, assure that the seating and props are as you requested, and adjust the microphone height, angle and volume level. If possible, take the time to sit in the audience, imagine being introduced and walk to the podium using your relaxed breathing pattern. Access your first few slides and begin the lecture so that you can adjust to hearing your amplified voice. Ask someone in the back of the room to confirm whether your loudness is appropriate.

Use an omni or multidirectional microphone, if possible, so that you can vary your head position and still be heard. Keep the microphone an outstretched hand's width away from your chin to assure that the P(Puh), T(Tuh), and K(Kuh) sounds don't pop. In addition to a podium microphone, I usually request a wireless lavaliere microphone to clip to my blouse or jacket which permits me to walk about the room. Always remember to turn the lavaliere microphone off when you visit the ladies room or talk to guests prior to your lecture!

Attaining
Speech Clarity

"Mumbling
Marsha"

"The rain in Spain falls mainly on the plain," begrudgingly practiced Eliza Doolittle in *My Fair Lady*. Television host Phil Donahue noticeably lisps on *S*, *SH*, and *CH* sounds and Barbara Walters distorts most of her *R* sounds. The significant success of these media stars, despite their near fatal speech flaws for average communication industry professionals, is a testament to their perseverance, motivation and will. Clearly however, Donohue and Walters are exceptions to the everyday norm. Speech clarity, including precise sound production, and proper rate, cadence and pronunciation, and elimination of "fillers and starters"are indispensable for anyone serious about improving her professional communication. Professionals from other countries must work even hard to master the speech and language intricacies of English.

I was contacted by a commercial realty company recently and agreed to train a supervisor they wished to promote to speak more clearly. Marsha was born in Nigeria, schooled in Britain and moved to the United States as an adult. Upon initial introduction, her imprecise speech pattern was immediately evident and appeared to compromise her self-confidence. Marsha freely acknowledged that her accent and rapid speech pattern required that she repeat herself often to her staff of over a hundred. She experienced even greater difficulty being understood by her superiors.

A series of one-hour training sessions geared toward decreasing Marsha's speaking rate were prescribed. We worked long and hard on her articulation, especially saying the ends of her words and correcting mispronounced sounds. Marsha needed to be retrained in stressing the correct syllable of words and learning to pronounce all the syllables of three-, four-, and five-syllable words. Marsha was diligent in tape recording her homework and critiquing her progress before the next session. Her vocabulary and ability to express herself verbally began to improve significantly. Before long, Marsha cheerfully reported that only on rare occasions did she need to repeat herself. Marsha was promoted and currently enjoys reading to the blind on weekends.

Actors and broadcasters are acutely conscious of the importance of crisp tongue, lip and jaw movements for clear articulation. However, most professional speakers have little or no knowledge of this. Most speakers attribute their poor speech to an inferior phone or inexpensive answering machine and frequently deny the prevalence of *uhs, ums,* and *like* as fillers and starters.

Try this! Call your answering machine and leave yourself another message. Also tape record a home or office conversation. Listen to these as before, but this time critically analyze your speech or diction. Ask yourself the following questions:

- Is your speech easily understood?
- Do you speak too rapidly, especially when nervous?
- Do you speak with a choppy cadence?
- Do you mispronounce certain sounds?
- Do you fumble enunciating lengthy words?

If you don't have any of these speech errors, go directly to page 99 and evaluate your speaking rate.

Acceptable Standard American English

"The keys are on top of the awgen" said Polly to the repair man, who had no idea what she was referring to. Ken went to the condo and found her keys right where Polly said, "on top of the organ." Polly had lived most of her life in Maine, before moving to Florida.

All humans are born capable of speaking any accent since our speech muscles and language systems are innate or inborn. Accents or dialects are learned, however, by hearing the regional speech patterns of those around us. Interestingly, a young child placed into any community will speak the local language without an accent, even if his parents have accents, says Steven Pinker, a professor and director of the Center for Cognitive Neuroscience at MIT. The ability to acquire language and a particular accent is related to age. "If you move to the United States after reaching puberty, you probably will speak with a foreign accent. If you move here before adolescence, you are more likely to sound Americanized," wrote Sara Mark in "Everybody Talks Funny," in a *Washington Post* article.

Often speakers resort to using their regional dialect when they visit home or attend alumni events. Donna finds it advantageous to use her regional dialect when she travels south so that she "fits in," but she will switch back to Standard American English when she returns to the Washington, D.C. office.

Accents in different parts of the country developed because of historical roots: the *pahk* for *park* the car of many Bostonians is reminiscent of their contacts with London. Norwegian and Swedish influences have produced the Minnesota 'o' so *out* sounds like *owh-oot*. Folks from the Eastern Shore of Maryland may retain remnants of Colonial English. Today, professional speakers worldwide speak Standard American English based on the International Phonetic Alphabet (IPA), a phonetic alphabet developed in 1886 in which a single sound is represented by a single symbol. For example the IPA vowel *e* in beef, brief, people, and Phoenix are all pronounced the same, although they have varied spellings. This is what makes learning to spell and speak English so difficult for foreigners and for Americans trying to neutralize or modify their accent. But knowing the IPA does help journalists and executives traveling to foreign countries to correctly pronounce clients' names. Further information about the historical origins of English can be obtained by reading Melvyn Bragg's book, *The Adventures of English*.

Fortunately, if you are unsure of how to pronounce a word, you can check a dictionary that contains the phonetic spelling of the word so that you can correctly sound it out. Better yet, web dictionaries list the word, the phonetic spelling and even pronounce the word for you.

The next section will provide a basis for understanding the 18 vowels and diphthongs (two vowel sounds that together form a new sound) and 25 consonants contained in the IPA. First you will need to listen carefully to your speech to determine which, if any, sounds are mispronounced. Then you must learn to discriminate or hear the difference between the incorrect and correct pronunciations. Finally, you can begin to produce the correct sound motorically. You will need to use a tape recorder so that you can hear yourself and a mirror so that you can see that certain sounds require lip rounding or opening.

Studying the next section will be a start for you. However, since accent modification is beyond the scope of this book, you may need to receive personal training by a professional. To locate a certified professional, check www.asha.org (the American Speech Language and Hearing Association) and www.vasta.org (Voice and Speech Trainer's

Association) and also the Yellow Pages of your phone book under "Speech and Language Pathologists" and teachers of ESL (English as a Second Language).

Precise Sound Articulation

Debra was an accomplished physician who was successful within the medical community and recently elected president of her professional association. Now almost sixty, she remembers having difficulty pronouncing her *R*, *SH* and *CH* sounds since early childhood and is frustrated because she never took the time to fix the problem. As spokesperson for women physicians throughout the country, she decided to undergo speech training. Debra could identify her incorrect sounds but had no idea of how to correctly produce them.

Using a mirror and tape recorder, Debra was diligent in pronouncing the correct sounds in words every morning and evening while on the treadmill. She spoke those words in phrases while looking into the mirror while dressing in the morning. She carried a small tablet with her and recorded words that she mispronounced during the day so that she could add them to her homework list.

Debra was overwhelmed at first because the more aware she became of her incorrect pronunciations, the less she wanted to speak publicly. Soon, however, her practice routine broadened to include phone calls and daily interactions at home and work. Recently, I received a DVD recording of her annual address that was expertly written and presented—without one articulation error!

Consonant Sounds

Let's start with consonants since they comprise about 65 percent of the Standard American English sounds. Consonants are created by our lips, tongue, lower jaw, soft palate, hard palate, and teeth, altering our breath to produce a sound or noise. Consonants can be made by stopping and releasing air or by making it hiss. They must be produced with some clarity or your speech will sound slurred and indistinct.

CONSONANT SOUNDS

Pronounce the following sentences containing consonant sounds. These sentences are grouped according to the place where the sounds are produced. The consonant *H* is excluded because no movement of the lips, jaw or tongue is required to produce an *H*. It consists of audible friction noise created as exhaled air proceeds through slightly constricted vocal folds.

- **Bilabials**–*B*, *P*, *M*, *W* and *Wh* (*hw*) sounds are produced by the lips.

A big blue badly bleeding blister.

Pam happened to slip when Pete put pepper on the apple.

Many million motorbikes from Miami came to the museum.

I wish I were what I was when I wanted to be what I am now.

- **Labiodentals**–*F* and *V* sounds are produced by placing the lower lip against the upper teeth.

Frank coughed and offered Flora enough fudge to comfort her.

Velda shoved Stephen into the vat with more vigor than love.

CONSONANT SOUNDS (CONT.)

■ **Lingua-alveolars**–*T*, *D*, *N*, *L*, *S*, and *Z* sounds are produced by the tongue tip or blade (middle of the tongue) on or near the upper gum ridge behind the upper front teeth.

The transatlantic train to Trenton tooted through the tunnel.

Do drop in at the Dewdrop Inn.

Queen Anne needs nine knitting needles.

Lena filled the pickle barrel with plump apples.

Sarah asked the cigar-smoking singer for the next dance.

Zelda was busy raising daisies in the zoo near Zion.

CONSONANT SOUNDS (CONT.)

- **Lingua-palatals**–*SH*, *SZH*, *CH*, *J*, *Y*, and *R* sounds are produced with the tongue tip or blade on or near the hard palate or roof of the mouth.

"<u>S</u>ure,"said <u>Sh</u>erry. "Let's ru<u>sh</u> the ma<u>ch</u>ines acro<u>ss</u> the o<u>c</u>ean."

The Per<u>s</u>ian lady pinned the cor<u>s</u>age onto the beige dress.

<u>Ch</u>arles, feeling ri<u>ght</u>eous, hid the ha<u>tch</u>et under the ba<u>tch</u> of pea<u>ch</u>es in the kit<u>ch</u>en.

<u>J</u>oyce fed <u>g</u>inger and <u>j</u>elly to <u>G</u>eorge as he planted cabbage at the e<u>dg</u>e of the lo<u>dg</u>e.

<u>Y</u>ank <u>Y</u>ork, the va<u>l</u>iant <u>y</u>oung champ<u>i</u>on, sailed the <u>y</u>ellow <u>y</u>acht that was loaded with bull<u>i</u>on.

<u>R</u>aymond could not bea<u>r</u> <u>r</u>ock and <u>r</u>oll music so Ge<u>rtr</u>ude w<u>r</u>ote an ope<u>r</u>a fo<u>r</u> him.

CONSONANT SOUNDS (CONT.)

■ **Lingua-velars–*K*, *G*,** and ***NG*** sounds are produced with the back of the tongue pressing against the soft palate.

Kate walked back into the cave after six members of the chorus ate the biscuits.

Golden eagles eat bugs and exist in ghettos during big plagues.

Uncle Bing sang the drinking song on the bank of the Lincoln River.

■ **Lingua-dentals–*Th*** (voiceless as in thumb) and ***Th*** (voiced as in this) are formed by placing the tip of the tongue between or against the front teeth.

Thelma thought Martha threw a booth into Lake Athens.

They saw father put the lather on the smooth leather.

How did you do?

Were you able to enunciate all of the sounds correctly? Did you notice that you substitute one sound for another?

Did you say the ends of the words crisply?

If *you did well!*

The good news is that you never have to actually learn all of the consonant categories since your brain knows from birth how to produce them, although you can't articulate them until your motor system grows. However, it certainly doesn't hurt to review these sentences or several of the tongue twisters or nonsense sentences listed at the end of this chapter when you wake up in the morning or before a presentation. Saying the ends of words enhances your clarity and can help to slow you down when you are nervous. Be sure to maintain your volume through the last word of the sentence. You don't want to swallow your last few words!

You may have already discovered that some consonants are accompanied by vocal fold vibration and some are not!

Put your fingers on your Adam's apple and say the **B**, **D**, **G**, **M**, **N**, **NG**, **V**, **Z**, **ZH**, **Y** sounds, not the names of the letters. Do you feel vibration in your vocal folds for all of these sounds? You should. Now say the **P**, **T**, **K**, **F**, **S**, **SH**, **CH** sounds and feel if they vibrate. They don't. Luckily, if English is your primary language, you know when a sound requires vocal fold vibration because it was hard-wired within you when you were born. Some differences in their pronunciation may exist in other dialects. For example, Arabic and Slavic speakers may confuse **T** for **D** as in *grant* for *grand*. Since a *th* sound does not exist for Asian speakers, they may say a t sound instead, as in *tink* for *think*. If you have consonant errors and English is not your primary language, learning Standard American English will teach you the rules that will correct your mispronounced sounds.

Vowel Sounds

Vowels are the sounds that we hear the most when we sing. If you place your hand on your Adam's apple and say any vowel such as *a, e, i, o, u*, you will feel vibration. Vowels resonate or carry our voice. That is why it helps to stretch them out when we need to speak louder. Vowels are classified by whether they are produced by the front, middle, or back of our tongue;

(continued on page 96)

IF YOU HAD SEVERAL ERRORS!

Locate a 6-inch mirror with a stand and place it on your desk. Look at your mouth, not your entire face, while you pronounce the sound alone ten or so times. Since sounds can occur in the beginning, middle or end of a word, practice saying the sound in the initial position or beginning of words first (sauerkraut). Once you have mastered them, move to practicing words where the sound occurs at the end of the word (justice), Lastly, pronounce words where the sound is in the middle (administration). The dictionary can help you to know if a *C* is pronounced like an *S* or a *K*. Say the sound in different positions as you drive to work. First, produce a word correctly and then use it in a sentence. Tape record your speech and use a mirror if you need to keep your tongue in or your lips rounded! Advance to the tongue twisters at the end of the chapter or make up your own.

whether the tongue is placed high or low; and whether the tongue muscles are tense or not. But, just as consonants are innate or hard wired within your brain, vowels are too; so you don't need to think about them unless you have a problem like Nadia.

Nadia worked at the Iranian Embassy and frequently returned to her native Iran where she was an acclaimed poet. She used her voice constantly, primarily speaking Farsi, which consists of many back vowels. She was beginning to experience a hoarse, raspy voice. Over time she learned to enunciate her back vowels and consonants a bit more forward in her mouth. This eliminated her very gutturally produced vowels, which had strained her vocal folds causing hoarseness.

If you wish to have a resonant voice, you will need to relax your jaw and tongue and allow the vowel sounds to emerge. James Earl Jones is a master at this. All of the vowels and diphthongs comprising Standard American English are listed below. You will note that each vowel and diphthong is associated with a certain phonetic symbol. You may need to refer to this vowel guide when using a dictionary to see how a word is pronounced.

VOWELS

Read each vowel and prolong it. See if you can tell that some vowels are produced in the front of your mouth while others are made in the middle or back of your mouth. For some vowels, your jaw may be more open and your lips may be rounded.

Front Vowels	Mid vowels	Back Vowels	Diphthongs
/i/ as in beat	/ʌ/ Cs in butt	/u/ as in boot u	/eɪ/ as in bait
/ɪ/ as in bit	/ə/ as in above	/ʊ/ as in book u	/aɪ/ as in bite
/e/ as in bake	/3/ as in bird	/o/ as in both	/oɪ/ as in boy
/ɛ/ as in bet	/ʃ/ as in better	/a/ as in bottle	/aʊ/ as in about
/æ/ as in bat	/ɔ/ as in bought	/ə/ as in bother	/ju/ as in beauty

RECITE THE FOLLOWING POEM

Silently at first, marking your breath pauses. Now read it aloud, focusing on stretching the vowels slightly and connecting the words between breaths. Take deeper breaths and pretend that you are reading to a group of thirty. You may wish to cup your hands around your ears so that you can hear your voice resound. Allow your voice to flow like Maya Angelo or Christiane Amanpour. Resonate like James Earl Jones.

Sea Fever
by John Masefield

I must go down to the seas again, to the lonely sea and the sky,
And all I ask is a tall ship and a star to steer her by;
And the wheels kick and the wind's song and the white sails shaking,
And a grey mist on the sea's face, and a grey dawn breaking.

I must go down to the seas again, for the call of the running tide,
Is a wild call and a clear call that may not be denied;
And all I ask is a windy day with the white clouds flying,
And the flung spray and the blown spume and the sea gulls crying.

I must go down to the seas again, to the vagrant gypsy life,
To the gull's way and the whale's way where the wind's like a whetted knife;
And all I ask is a merry yarn from a laughing fellow rover,
And a quiet sleep and a sweet dream when the long trick's over.

Proper Speaking Rate

"Lily-ha-so-much-she-wanted-to-say-tha-her-sounds-ran-together-and-i-was-har-to-understand-her-bu-she-kep-talkin (gasp) an-kep-goin-until-I-couldn-listen-any-more-an-I-interrupted-er."

We all know people who talk in one big slurred sentence with gasps to replenish their air. I am not sure if they just keep on talking so that no one can interrupt them or whether they just process information in very long units. Lily grew up in New York City and had a slight stuttering problem. She was an editor for a well-known Cincinnati paper and had skillful command of her vocabulary and language. The only problem was that Lily spoke very quickly and in extremely long utterances frequently comprised of three to four thoughts. Rarely could I, or other listeners, remember the content of her conversations. And, when she was passionate about a topic

- *Review the sounds of Standard American English.*
- *Say the ends of words to enhance your diction.*
- *Pronounce, don't swallow, the last word of an utterance.*
- *Resonate your vowels by relaxing your jaw and tongue.*
- *Read the dictionary aloud to practice problem sounds.*

her stuttering increased and she spoke even faster. Lily became cognizant of her fast rate and audible pauses by listening to portions of her morning phone calls for two consecutive days. She placed yellow sticky notes on her phone to remind herself to slow down. Eventually, her new speaking rate and pattern of breathing became automatic.

Your speaking rate includes the speed at which you speak and the length of your sounds and pauses. A speaker's average conversational rate is 140 to 180 words per minute (WPM). If the material is very technical or conveys sorrow or solemnity, your rate will be slower; approximately 125 WPM. Martin Luther King's "I Have a Dream" speech opened at a pace approximating 90 WPM, but ended at 150 WPM. If you recite a fairy tale, an amusing story, or are angry, your rate may vary from 180 to 200 WPM.

Read the following paragraph silently first and then read it out loud and time yourself. Stop at one minute and note your place. If you have finished the passage in about one minute, your speaking rate is perfect. If you finished it in 45 seconds, read it again and be sure to pronounce all the syllables of long words. Remember to allow sufficient time for replenishing breaths to occur. If not, your inhalations will be audible and you will sound nervous and tentative. If you read too slowly, finishing only two-thirds of the passage, read it again silently and mark where you think that you will breathe.

Practice any multi-syllable words that you couldn't pronounce. Then read the paragraph faster this time trying to smoothly link the words between your breath marks.

VOICE (130 WORDS – IN ONE MINUTE)

Generation of voice requires the interaction between respiratory, phonatory, resonatory and articulatory system complexes. The driving force of pulmonary air pressures combined with the resistance and elasticity of the thyroarytenoid muscles or vocal folds produces vibrations which resonate within the oral pharyngeal and nasal pharyngeal cavities. Sound frequencies are determined by the tensile properties of the cricothyroid musculature and the adductor movements of the lateral cricothyroid, interarytenoid and thyroarytenoid muscles. Hoarseness occurs whenever vocal fold adduction is affected by physiologic, structural, or neurological factors. Overuse, thyroid disease, vocal fold paresis or paralysis, lesions, inflammatory conditions, and laryngopharyngeal reflux are pathologies that greatly affect the voice. Diagnostic evaluation by a team of professionals including an otolaryngologist, voice pathologist, voice scientist and singing teacher is highly recommended in treating professional voice users.

Now read the following passage and aim for a rate of between 140 to 180 WPM. This should approximate your conversational rate of speech.

TAKING CARE OF YOURSELF
(163 WORDS – IN ONE MINUTE)

As we become older, time seems to move much faster which is illustrated by the feeling that Christmas comes the day after Thanksgiving. We must learn to slow down our world by acquiring hobbies that we enjoy, finding time to relax during the day and being mindful of taking care of ourselves. Many women find that playing bridge or joining a reading or women's golf group are wonderful ways to meet friends with similar interests. These women will quickly become a support and resource for you when you need a second opinion or helping hand. We must discover ways to relax during the day. This may consist of a walk around the office after lunch or stopping to perform three relaxed breaths every hour. Taking care of ourselves may be the hardest task to accomplish because women tend to care for others first. Being mindful of saying 'no' or delegating responsibilities to others will jump-start you into a more conscious way of being.

Read this thoughtful story. Your speaking rate will increase but your delivery should remain clear and articulate.

COOKIES OF CHILDHOOD
(200 WORDS – IN ONE MINUTE)

When I was four years old, my mother would bring me a cookie every time she came home from the market. I always went to the front yard and took my time eating it, sometimes forty-five minutes for one cookie. I would take a small bite and look up at the sky. Then I would touch the dog with my feet and take another small bite. I just enjoyed being there, with the sky, the bamboo thickets, the cat, the dog, the flowers. I was able to do that because I did not have much to worry about. I did not think of the future or regret the past. I was entirely in the present moment with my cookie, the dog, and everything.

Maybe you have the impression that you have lost the cookie of your childhood, but it is still there, somewhere in your heart. Everything is still there, and if you really want it, you can find it. Eating mindfully is a most important practice of meditation. We can eat in a way that we restore the cookie of our childhood. The present moment is filled with joy and happiness. If you are attentive, you will see it.

(Adapted from *Peace Is Every Step: The Path of Mindfulness in Everyday Life* by Thich Nhat Hanh, Bantam Books, NY, NY, 1992.)

Did your speaking rates for these three different exercises approximate the suggested times?

Now, refer back to the audiotapes that you've made of several of your phone conversations. Listen to your speaking rate and determine if it is appropriate for the situation. You may wish to transcribe one conversation and count the number of words. The tedious process of transcribing your chat will clarify areas needing attention. If your job requires technical presentations, extract 100 words from one of your texts and time yourself. Try to maintain a rate between 120 and 140 WPM. Tape record this segment and listen to it. You need to convince yourself that the rate that you are hearing inside your head is not as slow as it sounds. Since there appears to be a positive correlation between speaking rate and anxiety, it is essential that you become cognizant of your rate of speech when you are relaxed and when you are stressed.

Correct Word Pronunciation

Jane was a 40-year-old African American physician and researcher in a thriving university medical center. She was hired by a pharmaceutical company to record several TV spots for a product that she endorsed. Jane was born in Chicago but was raised in the South. Her speech appeared imprecise because she "telescoped" or shortened words by saying *gonna* for *going to* and *wudyathink* for *What do you think?* She also mispronounced words such as *"aks"* for *"ask"* and *"duh"* for *"the."* Her speech sounded less polished than expected for such an accomplished woman. Once Jane understood how her regional rules varied from Standard American English, she was able to correct her errors within several months.

Proper Speaking Rate Pointers

- *Calculate your reading rate in all 3 conditions.*

- *Pause sufficiently for replenishing breaths to occur.*

- *Clearly articulate complex technical words.*

- *Smoothly link your words together between breath pauses.*

- *Tape record and listen to several daily phone conversations.*

DO YOU SAY ANY OF THE FOLLOWING?

"expresso"instead of <u>espresso</u>

"heighth"instead of <u>height</u> (width and breadth are correct)

"miniture"instead of <u>miniature</u> (both the i and a vowels are pronounced)

"jewlry" instead of <u>jewelry</u> (the el is pronounced)

"often"instead of <u>ofen</u> (the t is silent)

"mischiev'eous" instead of <u>mis'chievous</u> (accent is on the first syllable)

"sherbert"instead of <u>sherbet</u>

"diphtheria"instead of <u>diftheria</u> (ph is pronounced like an f)

If you mispronounced any of the above or are simply curious, you can locate the commonly mispronounced words on the internet at sites such as www.yourdictionary.com and www.alphadictionary.com. It would behoove you to run through them and see if your pronunciations are correct. Cindy wishes that she had!

Cindy moved from a small town in Pennsylvania to the big city of Houston, Texas about 10 years ago. On her first day on the job, she was invited to lunch with her new boss and co-workers. When the waitress asked Cindy what she would like, she replied "*Qwickie*"(instead of *quiche*). As the table exploded into laugher, Cindy quickly retorted "and *vickyvoicy* (for *vichyssoise*) soup too." Everyone thought that she was a terrific comedian. Her quick thinking disguised the fact that she really didn't know how to pronounce *quiche* but luckily did know *vichyssoise* and could make a joke out of it.

Another common pronunciation error is "telescoping" or shortening the number of syllables in longer, multisyllabic words.

How many syllables are in the phrase "federal government?" If you say six, good for you! You would be surprised how many people answer four: "fed-ral govn-ment" instead of "fed-er-al gov-ern-ment" and omit syllables in attempting to present their message quickly. Speakers frequently telescope or shorten the number of syllables saying "nu-cler" instead of "nu-cle-ar" or "vet-rin-ary" for "vet-er-in-ar-y." It is critical that you clearly enunciate all of the syllables.

If your phone recording says "This is Sarah Jenkinson, administrative assistant to the Chief Information Officer in the office of the Secretary of the Treasury. Please leave a message and I will return your call promptly," in one breath, change your message. Speak more slowly and take a breath after the word *Officer* or *office*. A lengthy word like *administrative* has five syllables, equaling the number of syllables in "I went to the bank." So treat the two similarly and pronounce all of the parts. If articulating long technical words is challenging for you, read your professional newsletters and list your difficult words. Practice saying these words within sentences as you drive to work.

If you learned English as a second language, you may be misunderstood because you stress the wrong syllable of a word such as in saying, "I re-ser-VED a table for you" rather than "I re-SER-ved a table for you." This throws off the cadence of the sentence and greatly confuses the listener. This problem is rectified once you understand the Standard American

English rules for placing stress on words and can practice your problem words.

You may find it utterly impossible to say words such as *specifically, absolutely* and *surprisingly* when you are nervous and your tongue is stuck to the roof of your mouth. First, you must moisten your mouth by pulling the tip of your tongue back to your molars and biting on it — hard! This trick will always bring you saliva. It never fails to come to your rescue when your tongue feels like Styrofoam.

Second, prior to the event, practice saying the tough words to pronounce, tricky tongue twisters and nonsense sentences listed below. Rapid repetitions of challenging sound and word combinations will boost the agility of your tongue, lips and jaw. I strongly recommend that you say five of these in the shower every morning to get your speech muscles warmed up and ready to go. Create your own filled-with-tricky-sound combinations.

TOUGH WORDS TO PRONOUNCE

▓ sesquipedalian	malleability
▓ pusillanimity	anathematize
▓ legitimatize	consanguinity
▓ dystrophication	dyskinesia
▓ lieutenancy	pestilential

TRICKY TONGUE TWISTERS

▓ Red leather, yellow leather, lemon yellow leather.

▓ Shingles and single; shave a single shingle thin.

▓ Four frivolous flies furiously fought fourteen fearful fleas.

▓ Old oily Ollie oils old oily autos.

▓ Thirty-six thick silk threads.

▓ Chop shops stock chops.

▓ The sea ceaseth, but it sufficeth us.

NONSENSE SENTENCES

- The napkin slept and the butterfly glided along during the lengthy grill.

- Gardens of cement-grown wrought iron gates bloom in anthem-filled statistics.

- The absurd chocolate tart executive enticed a tranquilizing modification upon disjointed ant vehicle tongue twisters.

- He who peels parsnips today will eulogize snaredrums tomorrow.

Correct Word Pronunciation Pointers

- **Practice the 100 most mispronounced words.**

- **Articulate every syllable of multi-syllabic words.**

- **Warm-up your lips, tongue and jaw with tongue twister and nonsense sentences.**

- **Bite the tip of your tongue with your molars when your mouth gets dry.**

- **Maintain an on-going list of challenging words.**

If you can master these words, phrases, and sentences, your speech—even under stress—will be clear and precise.

COMPETENCY 5

Liberating
Your Voice

"Dull Denise"

Variety in pitch, volume, rhythm, and phrasing are indispensable tools for capturing and maintaining the attention and interest of your audience. Old time storytellers mesmerized their audiences with diverse inflection and variation in their speech. They were masters in timing the "pregnant pause," inserting it to greatly heighten suspense or accentuate the story's ending. You learned the basics of pitch, resonance, volume, and vocal range in chapter 2. Now, you will master the nuances of speech, which will enable you to captivate your audience even if the topic is mundane.

Denise contacted me because she could not project her voice well and did not hold the audience's attention during presentations. I was awed by Denise's beauty and statuesque posture as she entered the office. During our initial interview, however, she spoke in soft monotones, sat very stiffly and erect, and used few hand gestures. She carefully described her early education in a Catholic school where the nuns were very formal, polite, soft-spoken, and intelligent. I immediately understood Denise's demeanor. Denise headed the research division of a prestigious nonprofit association, where she was greatly respected for her input, but was perceived as too formal and quiet.

Training was fun as Denise, now cognitively aware of her programming in childhood, was able to unleash her restraints and become an enthusiastic student. We experimented with storytelling, pantomime, and charades to liberate her physically, emotionally, and expressively. Denise learned to saunter down the hall with a longer, relaxed stride, her arms swinging naturally. She developed clever openings for her statistics-driven lectures. She also learned to respect her facility for organization and made much-needed improvements in the structure of her boss's indeterminate departmental meetings. Today, Denise has much more fun at work and her children love their new mom who tells wonderful stories and plays charades with them.

Messages heard in childhood, such as "you can't tell jokes," or "just mouth the words and don't sing," can seriously compromise your future undertakings. As with Denise, they can destroy your spontaneity and spirit.

Are any of the following true of you?

- Is your voice monotonous sounding, lacking inflection and energy?
- Do people yawn or interrupt you when you talk to them?
- Does your negative "self-speak" prevent you from expressing yourself?
- Do your stories lack spunk?
- Do you pause effectively between ideas or do you insert fillers such as *um* or *er* before your next thought?

Liberate yourself by delving into this chapter. As you master new skills, cognitively restructure your "self-speak" so that old thoughts are extinguished and new positive conversations are created.

Effective Pitch and Loudness Variation

Marlene was an optometrist whose voice tired by the end of the day. She really wasn't that concerned about her voice, but came to visit me to use prepaid medical funds that would expire if not used within the month. Marlene spoke in a composed, boring voice, which she said she had learned in optometry school to minimize cuing the correct "Is it A? or is it B?" answer to patients. Marlene used a "different" voice when she counseled patients on her findings. She described her second voice as louder and faster, since she had 15 minutes total with each patient. During my evaluation, Marlene read a passage and mimicked conversing with a patient into a computerized software program that recorded and displayed her pitch and loudness variability. Upon playback, Marlene was shocked as she heard the monotony of her voice and visualized an almost straight line indicating little if any inflection or pitch and loudness variations. In training she rehearsed patient interviews and told stories into the computer while attending to the feedback and instructions to generate "hills and valleys" while speaking. Marlene's new energetic voice prompted livelier discussions with patients and incredibly more fun in her workplace. Her voice no longer tired by the end of the day.

Interesting Intonation and Inflection

The pattern or way in which melody or pitch changes throughout a sentence is referred to as intonation. It is the intonation that distinguishes the intention and mood of your utterance. Your intonation would be low-key and somber when reading a eulogy but very high-key and ecstatic if calling your mom to tell her you won $11,000,000 in the lottery.

Inflection refers to changing pitch within a sound or word. "*Who?*" uttered in surprise would have a rising inflection; whereas, "*Now!*" as a command would have falling inflection. I typically don't discuss these patterns in detail with clients, because if you are truthful and spontaneous, they will be appropriate. Only in the case of Jamie was attention paid to a rising inflection pattern implying uncertainty at the end of every utterance. This well-known and acquired "Valley Girl" pattern, which emerged several decades ago in the San Fernando Valley of Los Angeles, is rarely appropriate for the professional woman speaker.

INTONATION AND INFLECTION

Experiment reading the sentences below. The first ones are displayed in a unique way to encourage you to vary the inflection and pitch of your voice. Release your voice and vary the loudness of a word or phrase. Use your breath to keep your pitch lower so you don't squeak when you speak louder! Create your own patterns.

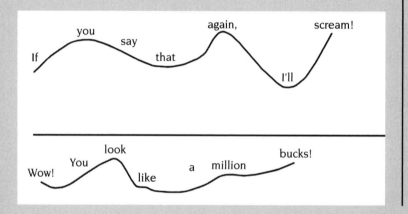

INTONATION AND INFLECTION

Read these one-liners twice. The first time, ignore the obvious emotional character and read them with flat affect, deliberately. The second time, read them with as much sincerity, vitality, and animation as you can muster.

How could you possible say that?

I would never consider it.

That dress is stunning!

I think that Iíve finally found Mr. Right.

Leave now and never come back.

You liar! I canít believe that you said that about me.

I love everything about you!

I despise everything that you stand for.

I regret that you missed the deadline by two hours.

She is dating my ex-husband? You must be kidding!

Emphasis

Placing emphasis on the important or key words of a sentence will create interest in your voice. Key words reveal the meaning and thought of your message and tend to be nouns, verbs, adjectives, and adverbs. Pronouns, prepositions and conjunctions are less frequently emphasized, although you will find exceptions. Use your voice to help the listener see, hear and feel these prominent words.

EMPHASIS

Read the following sentences and emphasize the underlined words. Did you increase or decrease your pitch and volume slightly? You should have! Try again, if you didn't!

■ When we persuade <u>others</u>, we often have to convince <u>ourselves</u>.

■ Is it <u>true</u> that though you can always tell a <u>Harvard Man</u>, you can't tell him much?

■ The sun sank <u>slowly</u> and was followed by <u>darkness</u> and an <u>enveloping, foggy chill</u>.

■ "Personally, I am always willing to <u>learn</u>, although I do not always like being <u>taught</u>." **Winston Churchill**

■ "A woman is like a teabag. You don't know how <u>strong</u> she is until you put her in <u>hot water</u>." **Delabian**

■ "Public speaking training is not <u>eliminating</u> the butterflies; it is getting them to <u>fly</u> in <u>formation</u>."
Toastmaster's International

You are almost ready to be the "despicable old hag step-sister" as you read *Cinderella* to your children. Read the fairy tale below with exaggerated vitality and animation. Picture your voice having many peaks and valleys on your computer monitor indicating your use of higher and lower pitches. No one is listening so have fun! Tape record your reading and play it back. You will be amazed to find that your performance is not nearly as outrageous as you thought. You may wish to read it again and exaggerate your dynamism three-fold. Then it should sound about right!

EMPHASIS

Read this silently first and determine where you will pause to breathe and which words are key. Remember to vary your pitch and loudness. You have been hired by the Discovery Channel to tell this story.

The Goose With The Golden Eggs

A farmer went to the nest of his goose to see whether she had laid an egg. To his surprise he found, instead of an ordinary goose egg, an egg of solid gold. Seizing the golden egg he rushed to the house in great excitement to show it to his wife. Every day thereafter the goose laid an egg of pure gold. But as the farmer grew rich he grew greedy. And thinking that if he killed the goose he could have all of her treasure at once, he cut her open only to find nothing at all.

Moral of the Story: The greedy who want more, lose all.

The Illustrated Treasury of Children's Literature, edited by Margaret Martignoni, Grosset & Dunlap, Publishers, New York, 1955.

Effective Pitch and Loudness Pointers

- **Vary the pitch of your voice 2 to 3 notes up and down as you speak.**

- **Emphasize key words with pitch and loudness alterations.**

- **Sound rested and fresh as you speak.**

- **Place a suitable reminder on your phone.**

- **Read fairy tales aloud for fun.**

Congratulations! You have proven to yourself that you can vary the tone of your voice incredibly well. Now comes the trying part. Read a paragraph from the newspaper aloud and vary your pitch two to three notes in either direction: higher or lower.

Emphasize keywords and use interesting intonation and inflection. Remember to replenish your breath when you need to and not at the author's punctuation mark at the end of a very long statement. Alter your loudness, either louder or softer, on key words. I strongly recommend that you record your voice and analyze it, so that you learn to love your new lively voice and despise your drab, boring, monotonous old voice. You are not changing your personality, you simply sound rested and fresh.

Place a smiley face or yellow sticky note on your phone with words such as *energy, be alive, smile* to remind you to use your new voice. Smiling into the phone really does add variety and energy to your voice.

Smooth Rhythm

Lyle Mayer, in his book, *Fundamentals of Voice and Articulation*, tells the story about Helena Modjeska, a great Polish actress who was once asked quite unexpectedly at a dinner party to do one of her favorite scenes from Shakespeare. She performed in Polish for about ten minutes before an English-speaking audience. Her performance was so emotional that her listeners were in tears. Later she confessed that she had merely recited the Polish alphabet over and over again.

I bet that you also have fooled a friend by sounding fluent in French, Italian, or Spanish when you knew that the message was incomprehensible. It was the rhythm or cadence of your voice that mesmerized your friends. Sounds in languages such as Italian, French, Spanish, and British flow smoothly in a connected way. A musical term for this is legato as opposed to staccato that is more typical of German, Arabic, and Hebrew. Typically when speaking Standard American English, we aim for a legato or smooth connected way of speaking, not a staccato or choppy disconnected mode of speaking. A staccato mode may be used issuing a command or providing explicit directions.

I don't recommend that you speak with a widely inflected pitch and an exaggerated legato as did Julia Child, but you do want to connect your words within a phrase. Typically, in Standard American English we connect our words with no pause until a breath is taken. The words, however, should be spoken clearly with appropriate intonational changes and the volume maintained through the last word spoken. Your over-all tone will be pleasant and your voice more resonant if you speak in this legato way. But, don't over connect the sounds like Juanita does.

Juanita called from Florida and left a message inquiring about vocal coaching. A few weeks earlier she had been hired by an established grocery store chain to make calls announcing that home delivery services were now available. Juanita's supervisors were complaining that her voice was dull and monotonous. Now, she was terrified of being fired, which also showed in her voice.

I listened three times to Juanita's message before I could clearly understand it. Her tone was monotonous, but the overriding factor was her slurred, almost too legato mode of speaking. I coached her to pronounce the ends of words and to articulate her sounds more clearly. As her intelligibility increases, she can begin to work on varying her pitch and loudness, which will add vitality to her voice.

You were introduced to the idea of connecting words between breaths in chapter 2 so that you wouldn't initiate vowels sharply. Now that you have a name for this smooth connected manner of speaking, you may wish to review the section on vowel sentences in chapter 2 and read the poem, "Sea Fever," in chapter 4 again. This time concentrate on smoothly connecting the words until it is time to breathe. Lightly saying the ends of words will prevent you from going too fast and slurring.

Smooth Rhythm Pointers

- **Speak in a legato manner.**
- **Briefly pronounce final T, D, K, G, CH, J, P, and B sounds.**
- **Connect your phrases between breaths.**
- **Speak with appropriate intonation and inflection.**

Valuable Pauses

We pause to replenish our breath, for clarity, and for dramatic effect. You should now understand when and how replenishing breaths are used in speaking. Remember, you are like a rubber duck bath toy that once squeezed bounces back to its original shape. Your breathing for speech is similar. You take a small breath and speak until you feel that it is time for another; and as you relax your throat and pause, the amount of air that you used will rush back into your lower rib cage … and the cycle continues.

VALUABLE PAUSES

Frequently, your breath pauses will coincide with punctuation marks, but not always.

Count from 1 to 50 over and over or repeat the months of the year again and again until you can feel when it is time to replenish your breath.

We pause for clarity and, more simply, where it makes the most sense. Read the following sentences out loud. This time pause whenever you see double vertical lines, but breathe only when you need to.

"Abundance is about being rich // with or without money."
Suze Orman

"Think of yourself as an athlete // I guarantee you it will change the way you stand // the way you walk// and the decisions you make about your body." Maria Burton Nelson

"The one important thing I've learned over the years is the difference between taking one's work seriously and one's self seriously // The first is imperative // the second is disastrous."
Dame Margot Fonteyn

Pauses for dramatic effect can be extremely powerful. A pause is an understated way of expressing meaning or emotional content. Pauses can be silent punctuation marks, offered after a phrase to signal its importance, or before a critical idea to heighten the suspense. Try to remember the last time a public speaker or actor had you teetering on the very edge of your seat awaiting her next word. And, the longer you had to wait, the greater the emotional impact of the message when finally delivered. George C. Scott once said that not only is the pause the most precious thing in speech, but it is the last fundamental the actor masters.

PAUSING FOR EFFECT

You can master the power of your pausing. Try these. As you read, vary the pauses: / = short   / / = medium   / / / / = long

- "To be happy / drop the words // if only/ and substitute instead // next time." Smiley Blanton

- "What is the most important thing in the world / / / / Love." Lyle Mayer

- "One of the most tragic things I know about human nature is that all of us tend to / / / / put off living. We are all dreaming of some magical rose garden over the horizon // instead of enjoying the roses blooming outside our windows today." Dale Carnegie

Now, read the following dialogues and vary the duration, pausing, loudness, and pitch of your voice. Be versatile. Be original.

MASTER THE POWER OF PAUSING

Fanny: Do you mean that? You're not just trying to be polite? Nick, I'm a good friend of yours. And in a dumb way, I'm kinda smart. So I'm going to tell you what you ought to do. You ought to marry me. You don't have to, I'm all yours anyway. But the kind of wife I'd be, you wouldn't *believe*! Look at my past record – no errors, no strikeouts, nothing! That means – no bad habits! I'd be learning the part fresh – *your* way? Besides that, I'm lucky! And I'd be lucky for you! What could be better for a gambler than a lucky wife?! Lennart, *Funny Girl*

Julie: You don't think I can stand the sight of blood, is that it? Oh, how I'd love to see your brains on that chopping block. I'd love to see the whole of your sex swimming in a sea of blood. The way I feel I could drink out of your skull. I could eat your heart roasted whole! You think I'm weak! My father will come home – find his money stolen! He'll send for the sheriff – and I'll tell him everything. Then there'll be peace and quiet …forever. Strindberg, *Miss Julie*

Valuable Pausing Pointers

- **Become comfortable with pauses.**

- **Pause naturally to replenish your breath.**

- **Pause for clarification of meaning.**

- **Vary the length of your pauses for dramatic effect.**

You are finally ready to tell your boyfriend, family, husband, colleague, or friend a story or a joke. Try to vary your pausing to add dramatic effect. Remember that the longer they have to wait, the greater your impact.

Reduced Starters and Fillers

"Like, I don't really know why I, like, called you. Um, I don't speak as well as, like, I should, you know..." said Jamie, as I listened laboriously to her. Twenty-seven-year-old Jamie worked for an ad agency in Alexandria, Virginia. She was smart, creative and a huge asset to the company in terms of her design skills, but she was never asked to sell her idea to a client. She wondered why?

Unfortunately, the "Valley Girl" generation which popularized the use of "like" several years ago is now in the work force and advancing this foible. Liza Sutherland, a 28-year-old sixth grade humanities teacher in New York stated in a *Wall Street Journal* interview: "I'm sure I say 'like' a lot. I don't worry so much about how my students speak." Sali Tagliamonte, professor of linguistics at the University of Toronto has researched the speech of the elderly in the United Kingdom, and found similar uses of "like" in 78-year-old women from Scotland.

This is horrible news! The younger generation may not care about using like as a filler in their conversations because everyone is saying it; the older generation may not be aware that they are using it. Even worse, "pro-like" supporters comment that the insertion of "like" gives the speaker time to gather her thoughts so she doesn't say the first thing that comes to mind. I'm not certain that this dispute is about the utility of "like" as much as it is about pauses in our speech.

A pause is an empty space or moment of silence between our thought units. We use pauses for emphasis, clarity or emotional effect. It simply may be a natural place to breathe. Often, we feel uncomfortable with pauses, so we insert fillers or starters such as *like, um, er, uh,* or *you know.* We may want to hold our turn in the conversation and need to use a filler, such as *um* or *er,* so that we are not interrupted. Perhaps we are nervous or simply unsure of what to say and need to start with something. Maybe it's just a habit. Regardless of the reason, if your speech contains too many of these, stop using them.

Awareness is the first step. I recorded Jamie during our initial visit and she graciously agreed to analyze her speech with me. She expressed shock, embarrassment, frustration, and extreme vulnerability upon hearing her tape. Fortunately, she was not videotaped, which would have revealed hair twirling, foot tapping, and head bobbing in addition to her many speech inserts. Once Jamie was overtly aware of her insertions and fillers, training could begin.

Jamie took this seriously and followed the program outlined below. Three weeks later, Jamie was thrilled with her improvement. She was poised and much calmer, no longer fidgeting with her hair. She spoke at a slightly slower rate of speech with assuredness and significantly reduced fillers and starts. Jamie continues to think "DUH" whenever a filler slips out and loves building her vocabulary.

ATTAIN A MORE PROFESSIONAL VOICE

Let's face this one head on! Jamie did!

Day 1

Record a portion of several phone calls ranging from your morning chat with a friend to a challenging business-related conversation. Listen to the tape critically and determine the nature of and reason for your insertions. Are they primarily starters because you are uncertain of how to begin the conversation or are they fillers so that you are not interrupted? You may find other reasons. Transcribing your entire conversation may cure you instantly.

Day 2

For an entire day, pay attention to your speech and listen for your speech foibles. Become totally aggravated by them!

ATTAIN A MORE PROFESSIONAL VOICE (CONT.)

Day 3

Early in the morning, as you are dressing or driving to work, speak for 30 seconds to yourself about your day yesterday. Speak simply.... "I woke up at 6:30 am and took Sadie for a walk. The weather was hotter and more humid than Monday. I came back in, fed Sadie, then I walked upstairs and took a shower." Take time to pause between thoughts. If you use a filler or starter, say "DUH" to yourself. Repeat your thought, without the "DUH" and continue speaking.

Have another monologue with yourself in the evening. Use more illustrative speech, "My day was logarithmically better than I expected. Fannie Mae is thrilled with my proposal and wished to commence training for its executive women's consortium immediately." Use improved vocabulary and try to paint word pictures, if appropriate, as in "the air smothered us like a blanket" and "the salesman fidgeted, stammered, and squirmed as I challenged him."

ATTAIN A MORE PROFESSIONAL VOICE (CONT.)

Day 4

Continue with your morning and evening monologues, but pick a more difficult subject such as abortion, the war in Iraq or the price of gasoline. Say "DUH" when you insert a non-word. Paint word pictures and expand your vocabulary.

Pick out three easy, short conversations at work. These may be talking to a colleague by the water cooler about the concert last night, simply catching up at lunch or calling for an appointment or information. Think ahead of your intention and possible unexpected questions. Breathe during the interaction and be comfortable with pauses. Think "DUH" after any fillers or starters. Don't become frustrated if some slip out. Be patient, breaking this habit will take time.

ATTAIN A MORE PROFESSIONAL VOICE (CONT.)

Days 5, 6 and 7

Rehearse communications that you have been dreading or ask yourself tricky questions and answer them. Do this frequently throughout the day.

Pick out one conversation an hour and think "DUH" if an *um, er, uh, like* or *you know* sneaks out. If you maintain a written schedule or list daily contacts in your Blackberry or Palm, clearly designate the interactions that you have chosen. Plan your thoughts ahead and pause when you need to. If you are unsure of what to say, pause, and let the other person have the floor. Put a sticky note with DUH on your phone as an additional reminder.

Week Two

You will know by now what topics, people and environments cause you to relapse into your old behaviors. Target these and plan for them. If you discover that people interrupt you, analyze this. Determine whether you are rambling or whether they are a Type A person who has to speak the second a thought arrives. Keep striving to build your vocabulary and expressive language skills. You may wish to log on to dictionary or vocabulary websites and review a page a day. Record a communication in the morning and afternoon, and review a portion and spot check yourself.

Pointers to Reduce Starters and Fillers

- *Replenish your breath when you need to.*
- *Be comfortable with pauses.*
- *Think "DUH" instead of inserting a non-word or filler.*
- *Build your vocabulary.*
- *Paint word pictures.*

DEVELOP A SCHEDULE

Get our your calendar and mark reminders so that you keep your goal in sight. Now, it is time for you to develop a reinforcement schedule that will work for you. You should be amazed at your progress so far. Since it takes 21 days to kick a habit, you are one-third of the way to becoming a powerful speaker. Congratulations – you're almost there!

Poised
Delivery

"Invisible Iris"

I lectured recently to a group of mid-career women in academic medicine. At the break, Myrna, an MD and associate professor, stated that she had no difficulty presenting clinical cases to her peers or research at a national meeting, but that she became tense and apprehensive speaking to her chairman. We quickly surmised that she prepares extensively prior to a presentation, but does not clearly outline her objectives prior to meetings with her chairman. She quickly understood that her timid posture, softer voice, and shallow breathing were due to her lack of topic focus and preparation. Once Myrna generalized being in her "presentation mode" to meetings with her chairman, her dilemma was solved.

Iris called me because her boss suggested that she learn to speak with more volume so that she could more actively participate in the firm. Iris was a senior sales agent in a flourishing commercial real estate firm based in Washington, D.C. She was extremely successful in her sales because of her relaxed and sincere demeanor. Clients immediately saw that Iris honestly cared that the property "perfectly fit" their needs. But, Iris was nervous and practically scared to death during the firm's cut-throat weekly progress meetings. Furthermore, her colleagues in the office did not value her easy going manner with her clients and also seethed that Iris left the office at 5 pm every evening to be with her family. Apparently, this was a source of unspoken contention in the firm. Iris described her boss and her female and male colleagues as competitive and unfriendly.

During her initial assessment, Iris decided that she would leave the firm rather than change her personality. She did not want the exhausting, hectic schedule of the other agents and valued her family time. By quietly observing others in the office, Iris realized that she possessed leadership qualities and might be able to change the ill will in the office. In training, Iris was able to decrease her physical anxiety during the weekly meetings, which provided her with the breath to speak louder. She researched regional and national sales figures for interesting data and began her weekly report with startling the team with statistics and insightful questions to the group. Presenting interesting data and topics to the group diminished her physical anxiety. The team began to distinguish her as a leader. Within several months, Iris was promoted within the firm to a more senior position and, upon last report, she thoroughly enjoys working with her fellow sales agents.

Once you understand the conversations and behaviors that undermine your performance, you will be set free to present yourself powerfully. Are any of the following true for you?

- Does your body feel shaky and your chest tight before you present?
- Do you avoid public speaking opportunities?
- Are you overly critical of yourself?
- Do you worry that you will look stupid if you make a mistake?
- Are impromptu speaking situations more difficult for you?

Calm Physical Self

It is well known and documented that the fear of public speaking approaches or even exceeds that of dying for many of us. We worry that we will forget what to say or that we will look dim in front of our colleagues. First you must recognize your physical signs of arousal. Does your mouth get dry? Does your heart rate increase? Do you become short of breath? Does your stomach get upset? Do you forget what you were going to say? Do you perspire under your arms? Does your voice shake? As I mentioned in chapter 3, if my nose doesn't run and my mouth doesn't get dry prior to even the simplest speaking engagement, I worry that I am not "up" for the event. I welcome these signals and immediately begin to use the relaxed non-speech breathing technique discussed in the first section of chapter 3.

Martha avoided public speaking at all costs. Even though she single-handedly created, conducted and raised $200,000 for an ovarian breast cancer research tournament, she asked a colleague to present the check to Johns Hopkins University Medical Center at the awards banquet. Her fear of failure paralyzed her. Martha never received the participants' public appreciation for her efforts, which diminished the thrill of the entire event for her. Avoiding such situations exponentially amplifies and reinforces your fear. What should you do to quiet yourself?

The moment that your arousal increases:

- Begin to use relaxed breathing.

- Breathe through your nose with your lips closed, relax your jaw, and place your tongue tip lightly behind your upper or lower front teeth. This will allow the perfect amount of air to enter your lower ribcage.

- Continue this pattern for three or four cycles.

Simultaneously, pay attention to your posture. If you are walking toward the podium or the front of the conference room, answer these questions:

- Is your breast bone forward and are you being pulled forward like a kite?

- Are your neck and shoulders relaxed and down?

- Are you gliding, swinging your arms naturally?

- When standing before the room, are you grounded with your lower body firmly planted into the floor?

Consciously using breath in this relaxed way will calm your "inside self" while you perform a "body check" to align your "outside self."

Calm Physical Self Pointers

- **Welcome your physiological signs of arousal.**

- **Begin relaxed non-speech breathing.**

- **Perform "body checks" frequently throughout the day.**

- **Voluntarily constrict then release tense muscles.**

- **Access your "performance mode" frequently.**

Perform frequent "body and breathing checks" throughout the day. If you are tense, consciously contract the specific area and release it. Daily practice will help you to diminish your body tension. Practice entering less challenging situations in "performance mode," indicating that you are attuned to relaxing your body, correcting your posture, and presenting yourself confidently. Become more familiar with your physical behaviors during demanding situations and pay conscious attention to your breathing. Slow breathing will quiet your body and get you prepared to perform. As you access this mode regularly, especially during challenging circumstances, your doubts and fears will subside.

Positive Mental Self

Diane had been a technical lead for SRA International, a federal systems integrator in Northern Virginia, and was thrilled to be interviewing for a project manager position. Although Diane was extremely knowledgeable about the project and a well-respected team player, she wanted to become more proficient in clearly presenting proposals to federal agencies and the Department of Defense.

During the evaluation, Diane was extremely critical of herself. As training continued, the more I commented on her progress the more she found wrong with it. Her reviews of her presentations centered on what was omitted and done less well rather than on her positive behaviors. Desperately, I asked her to jot down her critical comments for just one morning so that we could analyze her negative self-talk. A light bulb finally went on inside Diane and she asked how she could change her thinking. I suggested that for one day she be good to herself and comment to herself as if she was a little child. So the, "I was so stupid to forget that item" became, "I did a good job! I'll include the omitted item next week."

Self-talk is the running commentary that goes on in your head that continually assesses your performance. It either supports your behavior or negates your behavior. Emile Coué (1857-1926) was a French psychologist and pharmacist who pioneered using positive auto-suggestion as a healing treatment. Dr. Coué cured many patients by teaching them to repeat the statement, "Day by day, in every way, I am getting better and better," every morning and evening. This method, extremely popular in England and the U.S. in the 1920's, is similar to affirmation techniques used currently. An affirmation is a positive statement which, if said to yourself over time and with feeling, will change your thinking and your view of reality. Diane eventually advanced to repeating the affirmation, "I am a compelling speaker and perceptive leader at SRA International," every morning. This comment positively reinforced her behavior and energized her.

Listen to yourself and TRULY hear what you say. Is your self-talk positive or negative? Tackling the suggestions in this book will be hard for some of you. You must decide NOW to positively reinforce yourself, every step of the way.

Additional Examples of Positive Self-talk:

- When you do a body check and note that you are breathing naturally and gliding down the hall, say to yourself, "I am poised and strong and ready for any challenge."

- When you hear your nasal tone and modify it say, "I heard my old sound and was able to use my new voice."

- After you introduce a new colleague to the team, reinforce yourself and say, "I handled that introduction very well."

- If you mispronounced your supervisor's name, apologize and say silently to yourself, "I'm getting better at handling embarrassing situations."

POSITIVE AFFIRMATIONS

If you discover that your negative self-talk is hugely affecting your behavior, promise to do the following IMMEDIATELY! If you don't, you'll be working against yourself:

- Create three powerful affirmations and write them down. These need to be life-changing and a huge stretch for you.

- Every morning stand before the mirror, look yourself in the eye, and repeat each affirmation three times. In your head, you may be thinking, "This isn't true," but say it anyway three times.

- After about one week, these affirmations will lose their power. Create three more for the next week. Remember you are reprogramming your sub-conscious to change your thinking.

Kyo was an accomplished mezzo-soprano who graduated with her doctorate in performance from the Julliard School of Music in New York City and was hired by the Washington

National Opera. Last fall, she caught a virus which localized in her larynx and weakened her right vocal fold. Kyo was placed on disability for six months. Kyo's voice had been powerful, resonant and almost four octaves in range. After the virus, it was less than three octaves in range, weak and slightly breathy. She worked intensively to strengthen and re-balance her vocal fold, and within three months had regained normal function. However, her confidence had plummeted and her singing "wasn't the same," she bemoaned.

To counteract her predicament, Kyo's first three affirmations became:

- "My voice is stronger now than it was before."
- "I sing a full four octave range."
- "I am totally free and relaxed when I perform for others."

Her second week's affirmations were:

- "My sound fulfills my soul when I sing."
- "My upper range rings within the Kennedy Center."
- "I am a gifted mezzo-soprano and audiences love the sound of my voice."

Kyo recited these affirmations religiously every morning, and in a very short time she returned to the Kennedy Center and performed magnificently.

Positive Mental Self Pointers

- **Analyze your self-talk.**

- **Say loving comments to yourself.**

- **Create three powerful affirmations and say them every morning.**

- **Affirmations change your thinking.**

- **Change your thinking and your reality changes.**

Clever Openings

I will never forget the first communication seminar for women that I took about a decade ago in Washington, D.C., entitled *Powerful Communication Skills for Women*. In sauntered the presenter, a southern woman dressed in a royal blue, nicely designed suit. She stood before 50 of us and began to tell us about her grandchildren, all of their accomplishments, and how proud she was of them. Our energetic smiles diminished as we hesitantly glanced about the room wondering who would leave first. The matronly, nice grandmother then walked out of the room. Within seconds, in charged the same presenter with a big smile and captivating message. We understood the impact of powerful communication instantaneously.

Iris found that comparing her company's weekly sales to a competitor's sales, put her colleagues on the edges of their seats. They were primed to listen to the rest of her update and her anxiety about her presentation was basically gone. Whether you are presenting a scholarly work, a contract proposal, a sales pitch or a progress report, you have about ten seconds to capture your listener's attention. So, your opening had better be captivating. Several examples of openings are listed below:

Clever Openings

■ Ask a question

Laura opened a breakfast meeting last week by raising her hand in the air and polling the audience asking, "How many of you drank one cup of coffee this morning?" "How many drank two," etc. She then discussed how caffeine dries out voices and can cause hoarseness. Laura's hand raising exercise signaled to the audience that they should do the same.

■ State a startling statistic

"Do you know that over 50 percent of second marriages fail within three years?" Chris used this opening for a lecture to a singles group about the eHarmony.com Internet dating site.

Clever Openings (CONT.)

■ Use a visual aid

Lily showed pictures of the devastation Hurricane Katrina caused New Orleans, as the start of a fund-raising effort for Habitat for Humanity.

■ Provide an example

Martin Luther King's "I Have a Dream" speech educated the world to the realities that Blacks in America faced.

■ Tell a story

President Reagan was the first President to introduce the story of an unsung hero to the American people during the State of the Union Address.

■ Draw on a quotation or reference

On July 7, 2005 as British Prime Minister Tony Blair was leaving the G8 Conference in Scotland, after that morning's terrorist attack in London, he told the audience he was leaving to express concern for the families of the dead and injured, and vowed to continue combating terrorism.

Using any of the above suggestions will captivate your audience and also lessen your initial jitters about forgetting your opening lines. Be creative and design your own "signature" method. You will feel the energy that you have created in the room. Telling a personal story, or impersonating someone takes practice and acting skill at first, but your audience's reactions will reinforce your efforts. I guarantee you that even a renowned scientist with the long awaited cure for ovarian cancer will lose her audience if she delivers a dry, fact-driven lecture. Create your own powerful start!

Clever Opening Pointers

- **Ask a question.**
- **Tell a startling statistic.**
- **Use a visual aid.**
- **Provide an example.**
- **Tell a personal story.**
- **Draw on a quote or reference.**

Poised Delivery

■ Do you experience the greatest amount of anxiety when preparing to present to your colleagues?

■ Do you worry that their opinion of you might change if you slip-up?

■ Do you think that they know the information already?

Surprisingly, even the most proficient speakers answer a resounding, YES.

Joan was asked to present her ground-breaking findings regarding early genetic predictors of stage four breast cancer in African American women to the National Academy of Science. She had spent her entire career dedicated to this research, and, despite challenges by her chairman and several researchers in another academic camp, she had persevered. You would expect Joan to revel during her presentation at the sight of her detractors since her findings had become widely accepted and fully funded. However, she panicked at the mere thought of it. Joan knew her data inside and out but feared interrogation by these critical colleagues. Once Joan decided to openly acknowledge that these challenges had cemented her resolve, she spoke masterfully of the rigorous and exacting study which had resulted in her irrefutable findings.

When presenting to your colleagues or clients, be aware that part of your fear may lie with the thought of your listeners' passing judgment on you. To counteract this, know your subject matter cold! Research the topic as far in advance as possible and update it before your presentation. Decide what you want your audience to know and incorporate stories and data.

Prepare–Prepare–Prepare

1. Place your notes on five by seven inch note cards with key words and phrases in at least 18-point type. Be certain to number the note cards in the upper right hand corner in case you drop them! Never use a complete script. If presenting with PowerPoint, print the outline and use it rather than note cards.

2. Remember that slides are for the audience and not for you, so face your audience not your slides. A minimum of three to five bullets should be placed on each slide with a minimum 24-point type or greater. Several Internet resources for pictures and cartoons are Google.com (Advanced Image), Corbis.com, Cartoonbank.com and GettyImages.com.

Prepare–Prepare–Prepare (CONT.)

3. Stand and practice your entire talk at least two nights before the scheduled delivery. Record your opening and analyze it to determine if your speed is appropriate and your tone variable. Well-known executive consultants at Decker Communications advise speakers to use the 75 percent rule in timing presentations. Prepare enough material to last 75 percent of your allotted minutes, which will allow enough time for you to be spontaneous and also for discussion.

4. If a Question and Answer session is planned, prepare for the best and the worst possible question. Write each question on a note card, read it aloud, and respond as you would to the audience. On the day of the event:

- As the question is asked, jot down a note if necessary and repeat part of the question aloud if you need more time to process the answer.

- For example, if the questioner says, "Why do people in California continue to build palatial estates on the San Andreas Fault line?" You might say, "people continue to build huge estates on the fault line because ..." If the audience did not hear the question, repeat the entire question aloud.

Prepare–Prepare–Prepare (CONT.)

- If you are unsure of the question, ask the listener to clarify it so you aren't second guessing the question. You might say, "You are asking … is that correct?" or "Please rephrase your question so that I can clearly address your concern." You may find this technique extremely helpful during impromptu questioning also.

- If you don't know the answer, simply state, "I don't know," and ask if anyone in the audience knows. Not knowing the answer is fine, but don't get defensive or apologize for not knowing it. If appropriate, say, "That question is beyond my expertise, I will find out the answer and get back to you. Please leave your contact information at the registration desk."

- If someone in the audience disagrees with you and continues to question you, say, "You and I can discuss that for a few minutes after the presentation," or "Please leave your name and number and I can call you to complete our conversation later." The audience will appreciate your ability to move the situation forward.

Prepare–Prepare–Prepare (CONT.)

■ Don't be afraid to offer your own opinion.Women frequently underestimate how much they know and fail to trust their own opinion. Be wary of relinquishing your stand if, in your gut, you feel quite sure. It is far better to make a mistake than to continually second guess yourself. However, if you are not adequately informed about a topic related to yours, listen actively to the speaker, and learn about it later.

5. Don't forget to prepare a strong closing that will summarize your key points and, if desired, call for specific action. When finished, stand facing the audience, acknowledge the applause with a smile, and then glide away from the podium. Remember, you are the center of attention until you are off the stage!

Positive Audience Interaction

Accomplished speakers are able to interact and read their audience during a speech. I was asked to provide the guest lecture for a large women's organization in the Greater Washington, D.C. area in 1997. My good friend and fellow professional speaker, Maria Burton Nelson, was also attending the event, so I asked her to critique my address. She was very complimentary about the talk but commented that I did not pause to acknowledge the audience's laughter after my funny stories and humorous comments. Pausing for completion of their laugher signaled that I was really "with them." Not pausing implied that continuing my message was more important. I thanked her profusely and have changed that behavior.

Poised Delivery Pointers

- **Be an expert on your subject area.**
- **Prepare for 75 percent of your allotted time.**
- **Rehearse Q & A.**
- **Practice the entire talk two nights before.**
- **Close powerfully.**

The opening of your speech should energize and solicit your audience's attention. Then it is up to you to maintain and peak their interest as the talk continues. Direct your attention to avid listeners in the right third, the middle, the left third and the back of the auditorium. Maintain eye contact with those listeners who demonstrate engagement by leaning forward, smiling, or nodding in agreement. If someone in the audience is yawning or regretfully reading the newspaper, "look right through them." Ask the audience to provide examples and ask for volunteers if needed.

Pointers for Audience Interaction

- **Arrive 60 minutes early for your presentation.**

- **Interview participants prior to your talk.**

- **Solicit your audience's attention at the start.**

- **Clearly "read" your audience from the start through the finish of your lecture.**

- **Attend to audience members who appear captivated by your talk.**

Arrive at your presentation 60 minutes early, for two reasons. The first is to check the technical equipment and software to ensure faultless operation. The rest of the time should be devoted to talking to people registered for your talk. Learn directly why participants have attended the conference and what they expect to gain from your presentation, so you have first hand information and can design your presentation to meet the needs of the audience. Entertain, energize and enlist the participants to help you. They want you to succeed!

Expressing Yourself

"Reserved Rita"

Rita is a vice president for advertising with the top newspaper conglomerate in Washington, D.C. Well-dressed, poised, but shy, Rita came for training to learn to project her voice in large conference settings. During the initial interview, Rita divulged an extreme fear of public speaking and discomfort conversing in social situations with her superiors. Although Rita was an excellent manager of her staff and a top salesperson for the newspaper, in group meetings she rarely came early and spoke quickly with short direct answers to questions. She was hesitant to ask questions or comment during the paper's weekly briefings as well.

Rita was extremely self-critical. Her training began with increasing her awareness of her very polite, reserved posture and tendency to speak only when spoken to. As she learned assertive language strategies, she started to improve her ability to gain and maintain the floor during conversations with her husband and her friends. At work, superiors began to listen to her well-thought-out, insightful views and opinions. Now Rita soon became comfortable projecting her voice in group settings and began to arrive early to meetings just to engage in "small talk" with her bosses and colleagues. Rita expresses her views and opinions candidly at weekly briefings and is currently relied upon to present key issues. She is being considered for promotion to senior vice president.

Linda, a clinical nurse researcher, much preferred to quickly perform tasks herself than to deal with explaining procedures to the staff or trying to get them motivated and then reviewing who made mistakes and why. Linda arrived at her consultation with me completely exhausted. She spoke of working 12 hour days, which consisted of traveling to patients' homes to gather research data while also executing the daily nursing duties of her staff at the office. Her desire to avoid confrontation exceeded that of learning to assert herself. This tendency to "do it yourself" rather than deal with conflict is true for many women. How about you?

- Would you rather be liked than risk the challenges of management?
- Are you able to listen beyond the actual words spoken?
- Do you minimize yourself?
- Do you tend to over explain?
- Do you become defensive when criticized?
- Can you negotiate a win-win solution?

In this chapter, we will review the key components of effective self-expression. These include

- Listening,
- Using strong speech,
- Assertiveness, and, of course,
- Speaking powerfully.

Active Listening

True listening in a conversation involves an active two-way process where you attempt to emphasize and understand the intended message. If you don't understand the speaker's point, be honest and ask for clarification. If there is not enough time to listen, schedule a time to meet in the immediate future. It is very difficult to negotiate a solution powerfully if you don't clearly understand the other side of the story.

Pam, a psychotherapist in a busy practice, was concerned because Marcia, her assistant for five years, arrived at the office later than 8 am about once a week. More recently, the frequency had increased to two to three days a week. This created a major annoyance since Pam started seeing clients promptly at 8 am, and no one was present to check-in existing clients and complete the needed paperwork on new clients. Marcia and Pam had discussed this problem on several occasions, and Marcia's punctuality had improved for a short period of time, but then the problems resurfaced.

Pam didn't want to let Marcia go, but she didn't know what else to do. Finally, during a relaxed luncheon meeting with no time constraints, Pam achieved a breakthrough. She validated Marcia for her stellar work, then asked her for help in solving the "8 am dilemma." Marcia reluctantly shared that she and her husband had separated during the past year and she now had to drive cross-town every morning to drop the kids off at daycare before coming to work. With this information, Pam was able to work out a solution. They found a daycare facility close to work where Marcia could even have lunch with her children. If a crisis occurred, Marcia agreed to begin calling in a graduate student intern to cover for her until she could arrive at the office.

Faber and Mazlish write in their book *How to Talk so Kids Will Listen and Listen so Kids Will Talk*, that if a listener responds with full attention, active listening, acknowledgment of the emotional tone being expressed and permission for the speaker to continue, the speaker will feel less anxious and more willing to speak. It is critical that you listen precisely, with empathy, commitment and concentration, just as Pam did to resolve her aggravating differences with Marcia. Be certain to pay attention to your posture also. Be certain that your body language matches the intention of your communication. You don't project an open environment, if you are sitting back on your chair with your arms crossed as your colleague presents her review.

Sue Romero, a human resource consultant specializing in employee relations issues and management training, suggests that listening to the other side is the first step to successful negotiations. A comfortable lead-in statement such as the following may open the door for you: "I can see that we're approaching this situation differently. Let me listen to you first, and when I can explain your point of view, I'd like to communicate my interests. Would you be willing to do that?"

Using this approach can make a big difference for you in your daily and professional life. To be effective, you will need to be comfortable with pauses and able to articulate reflective comments such as, "What I hear you saying is," and open-ended questions, such as, "Help me understand why you have concerns." Actively listening to the concerns of others is the start to reaching a solution that satisfies all parties.

Avoiding and failing to address potential conflicts only heightens anxiety and can result in devastating consequences. What might have happened differently at Enron, had CEO Kenneth Lay taken direct action on the information that accounting vice president Sherron Watkins provided to him? During a a meeting where she presented the valuation scheme that Enron's financial organization was using to conceal billions of dollars of debt in dubious partnerships, Watkins wrote later, Lay seemed composed and genuinely concerned when he spoke to her. He said that he would have the attorneys look into the questionable deals. She left the meeting feeling, "Oh, good, now he knows." Watkins believed that Lay would take the action needed. As we know now, Enron's accounting fraud was massive in scale, but perhaps things might have turned out differently had Lay actively listened to Watkins.

A win-win solution to most conflict is possible, provided that both parties engage in an honest discussion of the issues in an open and comfortable environment. Your ability to actively listen and understand another's point of view without judgment is the first step. If you can "playback" the other person's view accurately and sincerely, you will validate his or her opinion. This should open the door for your opinion to be heard. The process requires patience and practice but it is well worth the effort. Remember, that your goal is to resolve the conflict that is preventing the real problem from being solved.

Active Listening Pointers

- **Create a non-threatening environment.**

- **Listen with empathy, commitment and concentration.**

- **Actively hear the underlying message.**

- **Use reflective and open-ended questions for clarification.**

- **Be cognizant of your body language.**

Strong Speech

In a recent speech before a group of female physicians, Karen, chairman of pulmonary medicine for Inova Medical Center in Fairfax, Virginia, introduced her topic saying, "I don't know much about this but," and then delivered the most profound talk on pulmonary fibrosis that I have ever heard! Unfortunately, her initial disclaimer diminished her power immediately. Did she wish to remain humble around the other female doctors?

Women frequently use comments such as, "it was nothing" or, "I'm not good at that but I'll try" or, "I was lucky to hit my drive that far." Something in our nature or our upbringing makes us not want to boast. I sometimes wonder if we are still in the "little girl mindset" of not talking about our accomplishments.

When groups of professional women are asked to introduce and say something about themselves, I've observed that they frequently talk about their children's or grandchildren's successes. Rarely do I hear about their MBA from Harvard or how they secured funding for a research grant on childhood autism. If each woman in the group is asked to comment on the achievement that SHE is most proud of, the energy in the room soars. The listeners delight at hearing their colleagues' accomplishments and quickly discover that their success did not take the power away from anyone else.

Minimizers

Disclaimers and minimizing comments ("minimizers") are remarks that lessen the significance or size of an accomplishment. They disempower you. Karen's, "I don't know much about this," or "I'm only an assistant," or "This is my first time speaking to an audience, can you tell?" all downgrade the speaker. Keep these comments to yourself at first and then try to eliminate them altogether. Try speaking in a declarative manner to a question rather than being tentative. When asked if the division will meet its goal this year, say "The division will meet its goal by July 1st. Our projects are two months ahead of schedule," rather than, "The division is doing well, I think that it might meet its 2005 goal." Even if you are not certain, speak your opinion: "In my opinion, the company is at fault." Rather than, "I'm not sure where the problem lies, perhaps it is with the company." These tentative statements are not "strong speech."

Promise that for one day you will listen analytically for any minimizing comments that you say out loud or in self-talk. Determine whether you use more of them when you are in the presence of a certain colleague, or when you discuss a specific topic. If you are on the golf course, you might catch yourself saying, "I shouldn't be playing golf, I can't hit this driver," or in a restaurant commenting, "I might as well have dessert, I'm already fat." Once you know what you are listening for, exclude these minimizing words. Say, "My drives are not working today," or "I'd love some apple pie for dessert." Be good to yourself and get rid of your critical commentary! If someone asks what you do for a living, empower yourself by saying, "I am a CPA for Fannie Mae," rather than, "I'm in accounting." Try, "I am CEO of my home where I raise my children and manage my husband," rather than, "I'm just a mom."

Overtalking

Jamie was a Ph.D. faculty member in the Department of Otolaryngology at a major university teaching hospital. She was disgruntled about the lack of organization and timeliness at the front desk and felt that the receptionist Carol was the culprit. During the monthly staff meeting, Jamie asked the faculty, "Is anyone having difficulty with the front desk?" She proceeded to verbalize her difficulties, providing patient examples, but never mentioned Carol. A few minutes later, Greg stated, "Carol needs to be replaced," and clearly stated three reasons why. The faculty agreed. Jamie wondered why she was not heard, the FIRST time.

Do you ever ramble, or feel that your thoughts are scattered even though you had a point to express when you started? I hear this all of the time. This is not such a big deal when chatting with a friend, but in a business interaction it is time consuming and can damage your career. Be clear and direct in your comments by simply stating your point and provide two or three reasons why. Listeners will appreciate your clear message and will respond to you, although you may feel that the communication is too abrupt and straightforward.

If you ask a question and don't receive an answer promptly, try to avoid the natural tendency to over explain. in her book, *Nice Girls Don't Get the Corner Office*, Lois Frankel coaches women to allow a message to be incomplete. Rather than continuing to provide the listener with additional information in an attempt to receive feedback, just be quiet and allow the interaction to be incomplete. If the listener needs further clarification, he can ask you. Think of situations where you have asked a question, and if you didn't get an "um" or a reply, you restated the question. More times than not, the person has heard you and is processing the response. Try not to jump to the conclusion that you were not understood and offer more information.

Not Accepting Credit

"You look dynamic in that suit!" declared Ann as Betsy walked into the conference room where she was to address the board. Betsy replied, "Oh, it's a little tight and five years old." Betsy needs practice in saying, "Thank you" or, "This is my favorite suit, thank you." If someone acknowledges your team for winning the award respond, "The team worked meticulously to solve the problem," or, "The team deserves this award for their solid work." Stating, "I never believed that the team could accomplish this" or, "It was a toss up as to whether your team or ours would receive the award," degrades your team. Comments that bolster yourself or the team are not arrogant or self-serving but vital to empowering yourself and the people who work with you.

Apologizing

At the pool party, I overheard Pam saying, "I'm sorry that the deviled eggs didn't turn out well," as the last one was gobbled up! Mary, at the weekly realtors staff meeting stated, "I'm sorry that the house on Klingle sold for $15,000 less than market value."

To the project manager's question, "Why didn't you provide these figures sooner?" Claire replied, "I'm sorry," when she had sent the figures to his Blackberry, as requested, the afternoon before.

It is far better to state the facts than to apologize. "The eggs aren't beautiful but they taste good." "I chose to accept this firm offer although it was less than the market value because the house needed much more work than the appraiser noted." "I sent the figures to your Blackberry yesterday afternoon. Would you also like a hard copy next time?"

Apologize when you are in error, but don't accept responsibility for other's errors or apologize for your less-than-perfect behavior. Pay attention to the number of times you say "I'm sorry" inappropriately. Chris kept track and recorded fifteen "I'm sorry" comments to the other three players on the golf course for her missed shots. On the next round, she tried to remain quiet or say to herself, "Keep your eye on the ball." She appeared more confident and was able to focus on her game not on "What will they think of me?"

Strong Speech Pointers

■ **Be clear and succinct in your message.**

■ **Allow feedback to be incomplete.**

■ **State your point and provide several reasons why.**

■ **Acknowledge compliments with thank you or a positive comment.**

■ **Apologize only when appropriate.**

Learned Assertiveness

Assertiveness training tapes and books abound. Log onto the Internet or Amazon.com or go to your favorite bookstore and browse until you find one that you like. Clients have benefited greatly from my sharing several of the strategies proposed by Manuel J. Smith in *When I Say No, I Feel Guilty*. I first read this book in my late teens and loved it. It provided me with tactics to use when my mom commented on my less than perfect hair or asked where I was when she called the night before. These two topics always provoked a battle. Mom eventually let go of the hair issue when I consciously agreed with her and replied, "You are right, I am having a bad hair day," or "I should get my bangs cut" to her comments, "I don't like the way your hair looks," or, "I liked your hair better when your bangs were short." Broken record or repeating a similar answer over and over solved the mystery of my whereabouts the night before. She quickly tired of my repeating, "I was out late last night" or, "I can't remember specifically where I was, but it was a late night!" rather than divulging my personal business.

Mara has been an information technology manager at the G S/M-15 level in the federal civil service for the past six years. Her new supervisor likes Mara's work and appears willing to support her application for a Senior Executive Service (SES) position, the highest classification attainable for federal employees. Although Mara possesses impressive technical knowledge and has developed a clear strategy to clarify some significant reporting errors for her entire department, she remains reluctant to express her ideas because past supervisors have labeled her "aggressive and stubborn." In coaching, Mara realized that she had failed to address small concerns with past supervisors powerfully enough until they escalated to the point where she then demanded resolution. After a number of sessions, Mara learned to use many of the assertiveness strategies discussed below to clarify misinterpretations and directly communicate with her boss. I look forward to hearing of Mara's promotion to SES next year.

Several of Manuel Smith's assertive therapy techniques are introduced below. These techniques will desensitize you from criticism so that you can actively listen. Don't get defensive, deny criticism or counterattack. Try them!

■ **Fogging**–Agree in principle, but you remain the judge of your behavior.

Boss: "You are always late to the board meetings."

Response: "You could be right. I have been late the past two meetings."

- **Broken record**–Keep repeating the same thing over and over.

    Superior: "The proposal is not complete."

    Response: "I'll have the proposal for you tomorrow."

    Superior: "You are always the last one to turn in projects."

    Response: "I will have the proposal to you tomorrow."

- **Negative assertion**–Dealing with valid criticism without apologizing

    Colleague: "You handled that meeting poorly."

    Response: "You're right. I didn't handle that argument very well."

- **Negative inquiry** –Ask for more information. It will help the speaker better define her comment.

    Superior: "That was a non-productive budget meeting."

    Response: "What about it was so bad?"

    Superior: "No one came up with any positive solutions."

    Response: "Why do you think that no one offered positive solutions?"

■ **Combinations of Techniques–**
Broken record and negative assertion:

> *Chairman*: "Your proposal is late."
>
> *Response*: "I'll have the proposal for you tomorrow."
>
> *Chairman*: "You always miss deadlines."
>
> *Response*: "You are right, I did miss the deadline, but I will have the proposal for you tomorrow."

■ **Negative inquiry**:

> *Chairman*: "Your last submission was not well thought out."
>
> *Response*: "What part of my submission was not acceptable?"

Learned Assertiveness Pointers

■ *Remain calm and in the present.*

■ *Desensitize yourself from criticism.*

■ *Consciously practice assertiveness techniques.*

■ *Rehearse being verbally assertive before an expected confrontation.*

■ *Simply respond to the facts; avoid emotion.*

As you read these examples, recall a situation involving conflict that you might have handled another way. Choose an interaction that you dread and rehearse the scenario, practicing these skills. Asserting yourself verbally can be fun if you remain calm, stay in the present and simply respond to the facts. Don't allow your emotions to assuage your power.

Adapted from *When I Say No, I Feel Guilty* by Manuel Smith. Bantam Books, NY, NY, 1975.

Powerful Speaking

"All my life I've wanted to be somebody. But I see now I should have been more specific," stated Jane.

■ Do you have a vision of how powerful and dynamic you can be?

■ How do you want to present yourself to others?

Julie, an extremely bright employee of the federal patent office in Washington, D.C. for five years, had recently been accepted to Harvard Law School. Her work at the patent office was comfortable and not extremely demanding. Applicants presented technical cases to her and little in the way of presentation or conflict resolution skills were required in her position. Among her strengths, Julie was able to process technical information very quickly and was extremely accomplished in determining and recommending which patents the federal government should approve. However, she was concerned that her introverted personality coupled with a very quick, almost unintelligible, speech pattern might cause difficulties in law school. Her fiancé continually urged her to be more outgoing and fun at cocktail parties and social events as well.

Julie came to my office for help in preparing for Harvard Law school. She was uncertain as to whether she would be able to succeed in the fast-paced verbal and social world of one of the nation's best law schools. As Julie and I worked to decrease her rate of speech, I urged her to engage in "small talk" with me. She immediately became unsure of what to say. She could respond to complex questioning about technical subjects, but had no idea of how to initiate or carry on a conversation at a social event.

Julie was disheartened with her progress until one day we were discussing the fact that brilliant yet introverted people have achieved remarkable successes, one of whom is Bill Gates, the founder of Microsoft. This was a revelation for Julie, and she quickly adopted the "former nerd" as a role model. Bill Gates's incredible success story became the inspiration that Julie needed to allow her to value her many strengths and overcome her weaknesses. Julie energetically learned to observe actively and ask appropriate questions in social situations, while better appreciating her introverted, introspective self. Envisioning herself as a female Bill Gates altered Julie's self image from that of a bright, insecure, mumbling patent analyst to that of a visionary leader with intelligence, empathy, and strong leadership skills. Julie will graduate from Harvard Law School next semester and now plans a career in the foreign service.

If you are like Julie and don't know what to talk about at a cocktail party, begin by observing people and things around you. When walking down the hall, look at the pictures on the walls and the people passing you. A boy is dressed in a football jersey, a woman is pushing her bicycle, and a teenager is wearing her dance leotard. Engaging in a social situation is easier if you realize that "small talk" is just that. It is conversation about the boy's football team, the weather, the city's sports teams, local news, national news, holidays, families, and the teenager's dance class. Be sure to read the headlines on a daily basis or listen to a daily news summary so that you are informed about the latest weather, news, sports, and style topics. Typical "small talk" in Washington starts with "Where do you work?" Small talk is intended to initiate a conversation; more meaningful topics are discussed as the conversation continues.

I ask clients to jot down in their PDA's and Blackberry's social data about colleagues such as their spouses' names, interests, children and vacations, etc. so that they can glance quickly at it prior to a meeting. You will greatly impress a new consultant if you ask him how his son is enjoying Stanford or how her vacation to Italy went. As your comments stimulate lively conversations, your confidence will soar.

Once Julie and I prioritized her needs, she tackled them in an organized way. She started with her weakest competencies—those of improving her conversational skills and decreasing her speech rate. Julie practiced her new voice by reading the paper aloud each morning and then leaving a message on my answering machine. She engaged in small talk initially with her fiancé and then with colleagues at the office. Julie's assurance and speech pattern improved significantly over several weeks.

Julie found it much easier to transfer her new skills to her everyday activities by choosing an ideal role model. Julie's choice of Bill Gates propelled her forward. She became the Microsoft CEO Bill Gates in Harvard Law and the philanthropist Bill Gates in social situations. Julie didn't need to think so intensely of what to say, or how to feel comfortable, she just became the female Bill Gates.

Remember Nasal Nelda? She chose Diane, a female radio announcer with whom she had worked in Chicago, as her role model. Every time Nelda recorded a news story, she imagined that she was Diane. Begin to think of someone who possesses the behavior that you want to emulate and who can be a positive role model. It can be someone that you know or someone that you know of and respect greatly.

Powerful Speaking Pointers

- **Create your vision.**
- **Use "small talk" effectively.**
- **Chose an exemplary role model.**
- **Pick a perfect negative example.**
- **Plan your next step and practice.**

I also request that clients pick someone who possesses the quality or behavior that they are trying to extinguish. Nelda picked Jan, a pesky neighbor in Chicago with a nasal voice as her negative image. If Nelda became nasal when stressed she pictured that she was Jan and immediately switched to being resonant Diane. Not wanting to be the negative image can be as powerful as desiring to emulate your positive model. Thinking about "Roberta" placed Julie back into the old scene of fumbling for words and speaking quickly at a meeting, so she could immediately change her vision to Bill Gates. I am not requesting that you not be yourself, but having a role model will help you immensely.

Becoming a powerful speaker does not mean that you must "save the world" or be an excellent orator or a silver-tongued negotiator. For some of you, it may mean simply reducing the number of *ums* and *ers* and being more succinct in a message. It may mean speaking with more animation and inflection. It may mean leaving an articulate, resonant message on clients' answering machines. It may mean practicing relaxed breathing in a meeting so that your report is presented in a louder, more relaxed voice. It may mean responding more assertively to conflict. Just develop a program that addresses the issue on a daily basis and get started.

Conclusion

You are already communicating more powerfully. You have read about the seven competencies and, even if you haven't practiced the exercises, I bet that you can now:

- Stand and walk more powerfully when you feel insecure.
- Note when your vocal pitch rises when you are nervous or speak loudly.
- Use relaxed breathing to calm yourself.
- Maintain your volume through the last word of a sentence rather than trail off.
- Speak more clearly and say all the syllables of words on your answering machine.

- Vary the pitch, inflection and loudness of your speech when talking.
- Notice when you use fillers and starters.
- Understand why your mouth gets dry or your chest gets tight before you present.
- Listen more actively to colleagues and family.
- Hear yourself saying "I'm sorry" and over explaining.
- Practice what to say when your boss criticizes you.

You are almost there...

But these new behaviors are not yet a part of you.

It will take 21 days of faithful concentration and practice to change a behavior. Mastery of that behavior in the toughest situation takes even longer. Hopefully you are now aware of what you want to change and have thought about changing it. But how do you remember to walk powerfully or breathe during a meeting when questions are being directed towards you? How do you assert yourself when you make a mistake and your boss is criticizing you?

First, just as Julie did, you must prioritize the competencies that you wish to strengthen. Pick the key one and work on it every morning. Let's say that having a monotonous voice is your problem. Every morning in the shower you should practice reciting nursery rhymes or a poem. Then as you are drying your hair, talk about your day and role play an actual conversation that you will have with your client later that day. Be sure to vary your pitch, loudness, intonation and inflection. Your voice in the real conversation later will express much more variety than it would have if you hadn't rehearsed the conversation earlier in the day. Be certain to pat yourself on the back and acknowledge that you were able to vary your pitch as you desired. Give yourself positive feedback about your success.

The next morning, choose a more challenging situation in which to use your new skills. With diligent practice and attention, these new behaviors will eventually become automatic. It may help you to put a rubber band around your wrist or a note on the phone to remind you to use the new behavior.

While you are mastering your new skills behaviors, try to use these skills in easier situations at first, progressing to more difficult ones. I ask clients to call my answering machine or their work phone every morning for a week and leave a message using their new voice. As this becomes automatic for them, they pick several more challenging situations every day. If you are working on being more assertive, for instance, have a friend or family member criticize you and practice using negative inquiry or negative assertion with them. Don't expect to be successful at first in an argumentative exchange with your supervisor, but I bet that you will be aware that there is an alternative to becoming defensive. After the interaction, you may wish to jot down the specifics of the conversation so that you can rehearse it and alter your response.

As you master one skill, move aggressively to your next weak area, keeping your momentum going. Remember to practice at least two to three minutes several times a day as needed to learn the motor skills taught in each of the first six chapters: whether learning to sit powerfully, be less nasal, control your breathing, vary your pitch, articulate crisply or answer impromptu questions.

Since I use my voice extensively on a daily basis, I warm up my voice every morning and every mid afternoon. This assures me that my breathing and vocal fold vibration are in synchrony with the articulatory movements of my jaw, lips, and tongue. The few minutes that it takes me too ...

> Hum a song in the shower,
>
> Lip flutter scales up and down,
>
> Say *meme* and count, and
>
> Recite a few tongue twisters

... keeps my vocal folds vibrating optimally so that I can speak with strength and resonance. You will find the exercise strategy that works best for you. Remember that these are learned skills that must be practiced on a routine basis.

The success stories I have cited in these chapters are real life, ordinary people who have invested the energy to do what is often very hard work. They have transformed careers and personal lives, as a result. Each wanted desperately to change, and each of them did through the application of the seven competencies coupled with practice, drill, and day-to-day application. You can too! But it is not simple and easy. In the movies *Rocky*, *Flashdance*, and *Chariots of Fire*, the sacrifice and pain required of the heroes before their ultimate triumphs may be extreme examples of what it takes. But the rewards are worth the personal investment!

Determine what factors are restraining you and change them. If you aren't quite sure, videotape yourself and analyze the tape critically. Use the seven competencies as a guide to know where to start. The moment that you truly make the commitment, remarkable changes will occur.

- Liberate yourself!
- Glide as you walk and sit tall.
- Speak with a voice that suits you and express yourself clearly and succinctly.
- Practice reading a dictionary aloud or reading the paper and retelling what you read varying your inflection and pausing.

- Use relaxed breathing so that the world around you will slow down.
- Use the "New You" in comfortable interactions at first until you can advance to more challenging environments.
- Write down three powerful affirmations and repeat them in the mirror every morning.
- Be poised and in "presentation mode" when you walk into the dry cleaners or ask the butcher for a pound of ham.

I guarantee that you will begin to feel yourself shift to a new level. Be cognizant of your goals and practice every day. In 21 days the "New You" will replace the "Old You." It may not be smooth sailing but the results will be incredible. Only you can do this for yourself.

Phyllis Mendel writes, "You have the ability to be a hero and the obligation to be a mentor."

Don't cheat yourself! Voice your opinion, resonantly. Ask for what you want, skillfully. Question what you do not understand, openly. Resolve conflict, assertively. Your daughters and the women supporting you will benefit from your exemplary role model. Make a difference for yourself and other women.

Be heard the FIRST time!

I'll be listening.

GOALS: TO IMPROVE VOCAL FOLD VIBRATION AND EXTEND VOCAL RANGE

Baseline: (Sept. 27, 2005)

Sustained **ee** or **oo**: 15 seconds

Lowest note: A2 Highest note: C4

EXERCISE	REPS	28-Sep	29-Sep	30-Sep	01-Oct	02-Oct	03-Oct	04-Oct	05-Oct	06-Oct	07-Oct	08-Oct
Sustain ee or oo sound	2	X	X	X	X	X	X	X	X	X	X	X
Glide from low to high pitch	2	X	X	X	X	X	X	X	X	X	X	X
Glide from high to low pitch	2	X	X	X	X	X	X	X	X	X	X	X
Lip flutter with sound	2	X	X	X	X	X	X	X	X	X	X	X
Lip flutter low to high pitch	2	X	X	X	X	X	X	X	X	X	X	X
Lip flutter high to low pitch	2	X	X	X	X	X	X	X	X	X	X	X

GOALS: TO IMPROVE VOCAL FOLD VIBRATION AND EXTEND VOCAL RANGE

Baseline: (date:)   Sustained **ee** or **oo**: 15 seconds

Lowest note: Highest note:

Use the blank exercise chart below to track your progress.

EXERCISE	REPS	DATE									
Sustain ee or oo sound	2										
Glide from low to high pitch	2										
Glide from high to low pitch	2										
Lip flutter with sound	2										
Lip flutter low to high pitch	2										
Lip flutter high to low pitch	2										

Selected References

Babcock, Linda and Laschever, Sara. *Women Don't Ask: Negotiation and the Gender Divide.* Princeton University Press, NJ. 2003.

Berkeley Susan. *Speak to Influence. Revised 2nd Edition.* Campbell Hall Press, NJ. 2004.

Boothman, Nicholas. *How to Make People Like You in 90 Seconds or Less.* Workman Publishing, NY. 2000.

Carnegie, Dale. *The Leader in You.* Simon & Schuster, NY. 1993.

Cooper, Morton. *Change Your Voice: Change Your Life: A Quick, Simple Plan for Finding and Using Your Natural Dynamic Voice.* Wilshire Book Co., Chatsworth, CA, 1996.

Decker Communications. *The Art of Communicating.* Decker Communications, Inc., San Francisco, CA. 1998.

Decker Communications. *Effective Communicating: Making the Spoken Connection.* Decker Communications, Inc., San Francisco, CA, 1998.

Faber, Adele, and Mazlish, Elaine. *How to Talk so Kids Will Listen and Listen so Kids Will Talk.* Avon books, Inc., NY, NY, 1999.

Fairbanks, Grant. *Voice and Articulation Drillbook.* Addison-Wesley Educational Publishers, Boston, MA, 1998.

Frankel, Lois. *Nice Girls Don't Get the Corner Office 101: Unconscious Mistakes Women Make that Sabotage Their Careers*. Time Warner Book Group, NY, NY, 2004.

Glenn, E.; Glenn, P.; Forman, S. *Your Voice and Articulation*, 4th Edition. Allyn & Bacon, Needham Heights, MA, 1998.

Heim, Pat. *Hardball for Women*. Penguin Group, NY, NY. 1993.

Horn Sam. *Tongue Fu! How to Deflect, Disarm, and Defuse Any Verbal Conflict*. St. Martin's Griffin, NY. 1996.

Jacobi, Jeffrey. *How to Say It with Your Voice*. Prentice Hall Press, Paramus, NJ. 1996.

Mark, Sara. "Everybody Talks Funny," *The Washington Post*, June 12, 1996.

Mayer, Lyle Vernon. *Fundamentals of Voice and Articulation*. 11th Edition. Wm. C. Brown, Dubuque, IA, 1995.

Miller, Susan and Berkeley, Susan. *Vocal Vitality* CD. Campbell Hall Press, NJ. 2003.

Mindell, Phyllis. *How to Say It for Women*. Prentice Hall Press, NY, NY. 2001.

Reardon, Kathleen. *The Secret Handshake*. Doubleday, 2002.

Shafir, Rebecca. *The Zen of Listening*. Quest Books, Wheaton, IL. 2000.

Smith, Manual. *When I Say No, I Feel Guilty*. Bantam Books, NY, NY. 1975.

Stone D., Patton B, Heen S. *Difficult Conversations*. Penguin Books, NY. 1999.

Sutherland, Lisa. Interview in *Wall Street Journal*. February 3, 2004.

Tannen, Deborah. *The Argument Culture*. Random House, Inc., NY. 1998.

Toogood, Granville. *The Articulate Executive*. McGraw-Hill, NY, NY, 1996.

Wilder, Lilyan. *7 Steps to Fearless Speaking*. John Wiley & Sons, Inc. NY, NY. 1999.

Biography

Susan Miller

Susan Miller, Ph.D. is founder of Voicetrainer, LLC a voice and communication consulting business. Dr. Miller has over twenty-six years of experience with professional and amateur speakers, radio and news broadcasters, and singers as well as extensive experience in major medical centers working with injured voices. She has been heard on the *Diane Rehm Show*, WTOP, *Georgetown University Forum*, *Derek McKinty Show*, CBS, and *Channel 8 Healthline*. Dr. Miller recently taught two six-week courses for the Smithsonian Associate Resident Program: *Cultivating the Medium of the Message—Your Voice and Communication Challenges in the Workplace*. Her tips regarding vocal image and vocal health have appeared in publications including *The New York Times*, *Better Homes and Gardens*, *Rock and Roll*, the *Washingtonian*, *Bottom Line Health*, and the *American Way*. She has appeared on CBS, Channel 8, and Montgomery County Television and provided 30-second voice analyses to guests of the *Diane Rehm Show* broadcast from the Newseum. Her recent CD *Vocal Vitality* was featured in the *Wall Street Journal* article "A Personal Trainer for Your Voice." Dr. Miller is a clinical associate for the George Washington University Voice Treatment Center and the Georgetown University Center for the Voice. Her passion is to empower all speakers and singers to become effective, compelling communicators.

Index